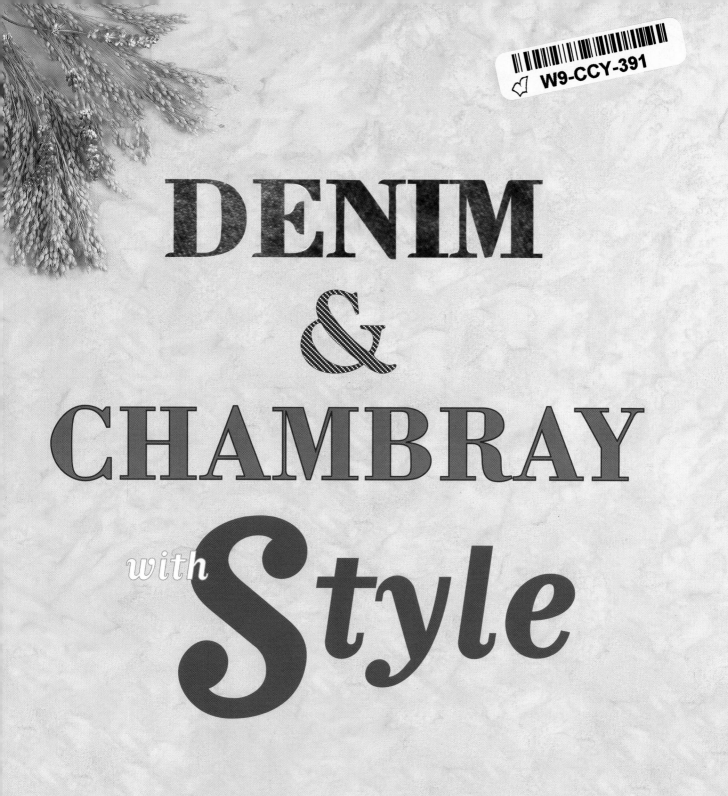

DENIM & CHAMBRAY

with *Style*

❧ Mary · Mulari ❦

Krause Publications
700 East State St., Iola, WI 54990-0001
Telephone 715-445-2214
www.krause.com

Please call or write for our free catalog of publications. Our toll-free number to place an order or obtain a free catalog is 800-258-0929 or please use our regular business telephone 715-445-2214 for editorial comment and further information.

Photography by G.W. Tucker Studio, Virginia, Minnesota
Illustrations by Mary Mulari

Library of Congress Catalog Number: 99-066539

ISBN: 0-87341-808-5

Printed in the United States of America

The following company and product names appear in the book:
ATP 505®, Aleene's Hot Stitch Fusible Web, All Night Media, AppliqEase™, Appli-Stamp™, BabyLock, Bagworks, Bernina, Brother, C.M. Offray & Sons, Cactus Punch, Clover Slash Cutter, Elna, Fabrico™, Fiskars, Fun-dation™ Possibility Panels, HTC inc., Heat-N-Bond™, Heat-N-Bond™ Lite, Hoffman Fabrics, JJ Handworks, Janome, Jean-A-Ma-Jig™, June Tailor Grid Marker™, The Junk-Jeans™ People, Kunin Felt, Lamé Leather, Olfa Rotary Point Cutter, OshKosh B'Gosh, Pelle's from Purrfection Artistic Wearables, Pelle's See-Thru Stamps™, Pellon, Pfaff, ReVisions, Pellon Stitch N Tear®, Sally Houk Exclusives, Schmetz, Singer, Space Tape™, Steam-A-Seam 2®, Steam-A-Seam Double Stick Fusible Bonding Web™, Stitchable Stencils™, Sulky Cut-Away Soft N Sheer®, Sulky KK2000™, Sulky Tear Easy®, Sunbelt, Tencel®, Tsukineko, Ultraleather™, Ultrasuede®, Viking, W.E. Wrights, The Warm Company, Wimpole Street Creations, Wonder-Under®, YLI Corporation, ZimPrints.

Dedication

In appreciation of the part it played in my sewing education, this book is dedicated to the 4-H sewing program, its leaders, and members.

Acknowledgments

I offer sincere thanks and appreciation to the following who contributed to my work on this book. I know I needed your advice, products, support, and cheer. To have such a network in the creative sewing business and in life is a wonderful thing. Thanks to:

The sewing machine companies and their representatives: BabyLock, Bernina, Brother, Elna, Janome, Pfaff, Singer, and Viking.

The manufacturers: Bagworks, Fiskars, June Tailor, Kunin Felt, HTC inc., Hoffman Fabrics, JJ Handworks, C.M. Offray & Sons, Pellon, ReVisions, Sally Houk Exclusives, Sunbelt, Sulky of America, The Warm Company, Wimpole Street Creations, W.E. Wright, and YLI Corporation.

The rubber stamp and supply companies: All Night Media, Pelle's from Purrfection Artistic Wearables, Tsukineko, and ZimPrints.

The new and old friends who offered suggestions, ideas, and buttons: Nicky Bookout, Katie Howell, Jolly Michel, Barb Prihoda, and Donna Rowe.

The friends in both my sewing world and my everyday life who express interest, support my work, and offer their thoughts.

The "Project Critics": Sarah Koski, Nancy Harp, and Barry Mulari.

The contributors of projects to this book: Dana Bontrager and Luveta Nickels.

Susan Keller who checked the accuracy of my instructions and made many useful suggestions.

The enthusiastic staff in the Sewing and Craft Book division of Krause Publications, and my project editor Barbara Case, overseeing with her calm and agreeable style this second book for me at Krause.

Introduction

The blues of denim and chambray are hard to resist. Most of us have a favorite denim dress or a well-worn chambray shirt in our wardrobe. *Denim & Chambray with Style* will help you transform that old favorite (or a crisp new purchase) into a one-of-a-kind treasure.

This book seemed a natural extension of my writing about sweatshirts, another kind of "comfort clothing" that continues to be a favorite part of our wardrobes. Like sweatshirts, denim and chambray garments are clothing pieces we value for their year-round comfort and versatility. We find it hard to live without them.

In addition to being practical, these terrific garments can be fun too! There are so many choices for personalizing denim and chambray. Make a dramatic statement with extensive embellishment or create a subtle change with a small accent. A geometric applique over the pocket of a man's denim shirt gives a distinctive mark of style to office wear for "Casual Friday." Handkerchief corners wrapped around the neckline and front edge of a jumper restyle the plain garment. A change of buttons inspires applique designs to match the colors and style of the new buttons on a denim top.

My sisters and I - The Koski girls together in denim - Ruth, Rachel, Mary, Becky, and Sarah.

Read through the Table of Contents or page through the book to see pictures and close-ups of the many clever details that can be added to purchased denim and chambray clothing. (Of course, if you prefer, you can sew the clothing yourself.) Each project includes complete instructions for adding accents to existing garments. Some can be done in an afternoon; others are a little more involved. Most require only basic sewing skills and a machine. Several projects don't require any sewing.

Don't forget that the decorating ideas presented here work on other clothing too. Take time to check out other unadorned garments in your closet - they may be candidates for improvement and enhancement with the decorating techniques you'll learn from this book. You'll find many ways to salvage portions of old jeans for embellishment, so be sure to save at least one pair that is stained, torn, or no longer fits.

In all my books, I recommend that readers add their own notes in the margins and open spaces (assuming, of course, that you're not borrowing the book from the library!). Also consider taking the book to a print shop where a spiral binding can be added. A book that lies flat on your sewing room table will be appreciated each time you work on a project.

As an author, teacher, and one who shares her ideas, I encourage you to share your thoughts, ideas, and inspirations with me. Please write to me at Mary's Productions, Box 87-K2, Aurora, MN 55705. It's always interesting to hear from readers and sewing enthusiasts who use my books. Let me know how you have used and altered my ideas.

Now on to the pleasures of adding sewing style to denim and chambray!

Mary Mulari

Before

After

Table of Contents

About Denim & Chambray

Denim and chambray have become essential year-round fabrics in our wardrobes. They are our "comfort clothes," they blend with other colors and styles, and they've become acceptable and suitable for nearly any occasion. Fabrics once worn only by cowboys, farmers, and construction workers now appear in offices, in wedding attire, and on people of all ages and lifestyles.

Denim had its beginnings in Europe. In Nimes, France, wool twill fabric was named "serge de Nimes" and that may be where the name "denim" originated. "Sergedenim" became a cotton twill fabric in the late 1700s and was produced in England. From there it came to America where it was produced as a fabric for working people. Both the Europeans and Americans appreciated its comfort, durability, economy, and washability. The same features are appreciated today.

It's no wonder we have fallen in love with denim. The fabric has so many desirable qualities - it is durable and hardy, yet soft and flexible. These features are due to the way it is made. The lengthwise yarns (warp threads) of denim are dyed blue before they are woven. The crosswise yarns (weft threads) are the filling yarn and they are undyed. The blue yarns show on the right side of the fabric and the natural colored yarns make the wrong side of the fabric much lighter or white. Chambray is also manufactured as a yarn-dyed cloth with white or unbleached threads crossing colored warp threads.

The popularity of denim and chambray in clothing has led to use in accessories, home decor, shoes, and more. Both denim and chambray are available in different weights and in prewashed conditions. New fabrics like Tencel duplicate the color and the style of denim with other natural fibers. We just can't seem to get enough denim in our lives.

It's a natural move then to personalize our denim and chambray garments with other fabrics, yarns, buttons, and even old tablecloths. With just basic sewing skills we can improve our clothing to be even more comfortable, one-of-a-kind garments with a mark of style. Start with your closet and gather up all the denim and chambray you can. Then turn the page to find the perfect projects to rejuvenate your comfort clothes.

Information collected from Cone Denim website (www.cone.com) in February 1999 and "From Crusades to Cultural Icon, The lesser-known history of denim" by Rebecca Raether in Lands' End catalog (Lands' End, 1 Lands' End Lane, Dodgeville, WI 53595), Feb. 1999, pages 44-45.

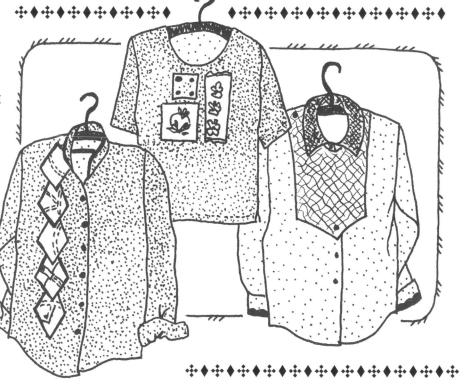

Frequently Used Supplies & Equipment

As you check the "Supplies to Gather" at the beginning of each project, you'll find that many items appear in list after list. To save time, this chapter offers information about these products, and the reasoning behind using them. The more you use these items, the more often you'll turn to them in a variety of sewing situations.

Check your sewing room supply box and/or visit your favorite sewing store to make sure you have these products on hand.

MARKERS & PENS

Chalk Marker - This tool makes it easy to mark lines that can be seen on dark or medium denim fabrics and some chambrays too. The marks are easy to brush off

Supply Basket
An easy-to-find collection of supplies used for the projects in this book will save time when you're ready to sew.

afterwards in the event you haven't covered them with sewing. The markers come as triangles of smooth chalk or chalk applicators. Either variety works well.

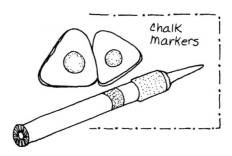

Wash-Away Marking Pens - This type of marker has a sharp point and marks clearly on chambray or lighter denim fabrics. Marks made by the blue-tipped marker will disappear with water, and the purple variety disappears on its own after three days or even sooner if the weather is humid. For sewing you want to do *right now*, the purple marker is a great choice. Just don't expect the lines you mark to show if you're away from your sewing for several days. And don't use purple to mark the route on a map for a trip you plan to take in two weeks!

NEEDLES & THREADS

Denim Needles - These specialty needles are equipped with a sharp point to sew dense fabrics like denim. Many of the projects in this book require that you sew extra layers of fabric onto denim. It's a good idea to use a sewing needle that will accommodate the fabric you've chosen to sew on. These needles are distinguished by the blue shank so you can easily identify which needle is on the machine.

Double Needles - The size of these specialty needles refers to the distance between the two needles, which are attached to a bar and a single shank that fits on the machine. For example, 6.0 means that the two needles are 6 millimeters apart; this is considered an extra-wide double needle, so your machine must be

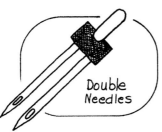

Double Needles

able to stitch a 6.5mm zigzag to use it. Specialty denim needles are available in a 4.0 double needle size.

Generally, most people think of sewing straight stitches with a double needle, but there are many other stitches that are interesting to try. Before exploring the double needle's versatility, press the double needle safety button on your sewing machine (if there is one). Also, always hand-turn the hand wheel slowly, watching the needles swing from side to side to make sure they don't strike either the presser foot or the bed of the machine, which would cause them to break.

Topstitch Needle - The size of the eye of this needle allows for thicker thread or more than one thinner thread to pass through to the fabric and form good stitches. The needle also does not pierce large holes in fabrics. It's always good advice to sew slowly with thicker threads and the topstitch needle; the results will be worth a little of your patience.

Clear Nylon Threads - You'll see this product listed many times. There are two varieties: clear and smoke. For stitching on dark fabrics, the smoke thread (which looks dark gray on the spool) blends best. For lighter colors, use the clear variety. I used these threads frequently as I prepared the sample garments for this book and sewed on many different colors of fabric in one project. In the bobbin, use standard sewing thread in a neutral color that blends with the denim fabrics, such as dusty blue or gray, or use black or white bobbin thread.

Jeans Thread by YLI - The first color available in this thread was gold, to match blue jeans stitching thread. It is 100% polyester thread in 30 weight. Now a great variety of colors and variegated colors are available and I've used them to embellish many of the projects in this book. This could be a good opportunity for you to experiment, learn about, and appreciate a new thread. Be sure to use a topstitching needle with this thread.

FUSIBLES & STABILIZERS

Paper-Backed Fusible Web - The first one of these on the market was Wonder-Under but others such as Heat-N-Bond Lite and Aleene's Hot Stitch Fusible Web soon followed. These products revolutionized applique by offering us a way to fuse and hold all edges of a design to the fabric on which it would be sewn. Now there's no problem with a design shifting or gaping as we sew around it. See the applique instructions in the Workshop section on page 120 for detailed use of this product category. Be sure to use the sew-through varieties of paper-backed fusible webs when you plan to sew around appliques. The other types, such as Heat-N-Bond Regular and Heavy Duty Wonder-Under, are made for no-sew projects and will cause problems with sewing machine needles if you try to sew through them.

Double Stick Paper-Backed Fusible Web - Two product brands fit this category: Steam-A-Seam 2 and AppliqEase. They are different from regular paper-backed fusible web products because two layers of paper cover the fusible web. By removing one layer of paper, finger pressing the product to the wrong side of fabric, then removing the second layer of paper, you create a fabric piece that is tacky on one side and can be moved from one spot to another to test design placement locations. This feature offers a convenient way to change your mind and move fabrics and designs around. Once you've chosen the correct location for designs (or bias tape or other strips of trim), simply fuse them in place and sew around the edges. Refer to the product information that comes with the product for iron temperature, etc. The fusing material does not gum up the sewing machine needle.

Fusible Spray - Sulky KK2000 and ATP 505 are two brands of this product. When sprayed to the wrong side of an applique or other embellishment, this spray makes the back of the applique sticky to the touch. The word "temporary" is key here because the spray does not replace sewing - it holds designs in place while you sew. On many projects, you can use it instead of paper-backed fusible webs and avoid the extra layer of thickness they add to a design. Once you get in the habit of using them, you'll find that fusible sprays are indispensable in your sewing room.

Fusible Interfacing - Parts of some fabrics in the projects need a bit of stabilizing or an extra layer to prevent seeing through an applique, especially if it is placed on a dark denim garment. My preference in lightweight fusible interfacing is the tricot knit variety, which is available in white, black, or gray. If one layer is not enough, fuse on a second layer. This product does not stiffen the fabric but gives it extra body and stability.

Stabilizers - Even though many denim fabrics are very dense and stable, it is important to use a stabilizer beneath the fabric while you are stitching. Many times it will be a tear-away variety that is removed after the stitching is completed. Be careful about ripping too enthusiastically and distorting or pulling out stitches. If you find this to be a problem for you, cut away the excess stabilizer and leave the rest under the stitching to act as a support. There are several kinds of cut-away stabilizers that are soft enough to be left on the back of the fabric. One example, Sulky Cut-Away Soft N Sheer, comes in both white and black. The black color often blends better with denims.

OTHER TOOLS & NOTIONS

Rotary Cutter, Mat and Ruler - Using a rotary cutter on fabric produces clean edges and offers a fast way to cut. Invest in a scallop or wavy edge blade and learn to use your cutter for decorative purposes with nonfray fabrics.

Bodkin - For lacing trim through openings on a garment and for sliding cording through a casing, you just can't beat a bodkin. This simple tool grasps the end of a strip in its notched end while the opposite rounded smooth end slides through the openings. It's much better than using a large safety pin!

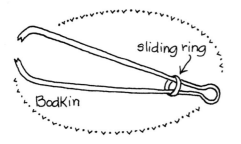

sliding ring

Bodkin

Templates - I have found a set of clear plastic circle and square templates to be wonderful sewing tools. You can see through the template for design placement or trace around the firm edges to draw denim circles for Denim Chrysanthemums (page 40) and other projects in this book. If you don't already have templates, one way to improvise is to carefully cut circles from quilting template plastic. Just remember that word "carefully."

Mesh Laundry Bag - Zip all your denim cutting experiments in a mesh bag and they're all consolidated in one place. No more loose threads of fabric and twisted strips circulating in the washer and dryer and entwining with other clothing. In my laundry room, mesh bags are also used for new fabrics I want to prewash. They isolate the fabrics and eliminate that mass of threads tangling the fabrics and attaching them to the agitator of the washing machine! Know what I'm talking about? Mesh bags help in the dryer too.

Mesh Bag

Button Collection - Many times you will see the suggestion to change the buttons on a denim or chambray garment. Once you try this and see the difference better buttons make on clothing, you'll be making this change often. If you have a button stash, dig through and choose charming old buttons to make your garment "new." If you're lucky enough to have access to a store with great new buttons, consider yourself very fortunate, and make sure to support that business with frequent button purchases. Tell your friends too!

WEAVING, COUCHING & STITCHING FOR TEXTURE

cutwork jumper yoke

Seminole patchwork

denim blazer with style

weaving through denim

Sashiko style topstitch

between the pintucks

Cutwork Jumper Yoke

Achieve the look of weaving by stitching a second fabric to the wrong side of a denim garment and then cutting away sections of the denim to reveal the second fabric beneath. I chose a dark denim jumper and an interesting blue shaded dishtowel for the back layer of fabric. Look for this jumper on my sister Rachel in our family picture on page 4.

Cutwork Jumper Yoke

The blue and white dishtowel used as the decorative fabric revealed by the cutwork is shown under the birch log. You'll see my sister Rachel wearing this jumper in our family photo. She's the youngest in the family and as a toddler, she would cheer as the rest of us got on the school bus because she could stay home to wash the dishes. This dishtowel project was perfect for her to wear!

Supplies to Gather:

Denim jumper with plain front

1/2 to 1 yd. fabric for layering, or 1 dishtowel

Top thread to match or contrast with denim garment

Chalk marker

Optional: lightweight fusible interfacing

Steps to Take:

1. Select the area of the garment that you want to layer with cutwork. Don't limit yourself to the jumper idea featured. Consider using this technique on one or both shirt fronts, a back yoke of a dress or shirt, or the hemline area of a dress.

2. With a chalk marker, draw the outline of the design area on the garment. (Fig. 1) Make a tracing or tissue paper copy of the area.

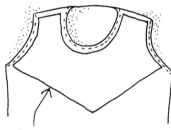

Chalk marking of design outline on front of jumper

Fig. 1

3. Cut the piece of fabric for the backing layer 3/4" larger than the actual design area. If the fabric is soft and could use more stability, fuse interfacing to the wrong side. Zigzag or serge the edges of the fabric. (Fig. 2)

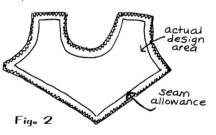

actual design area

seam allowance

Fig. 2

4. Pin the backing fabric to the garment so the right side faces the wrong side of the garment. Use many pins, or, for an even more stable hold, baste the piece to the garment.

5. Using your matching top thread, straight stitch around the edge of the design area marked in chalk on the garment.

6. Using a chalk marker, draw a grid within the area of the design section. I chose to draw curving lines on the jumper yoke rather than straight lines. (Fig. 3)

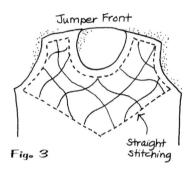

Jumper Front

Straight Stitching

Fig. 3

7. Using your matching top thread and a medium to wide width satin stitch (3.0 to 4.0), satin stitch on the lines inside the design area. The final satin stitching will cover the outline straight stitching you did earlier. Remove the pins.

8. Chalk mark an X on the sections of the top fabric you plan to cut out. It's easy to lose track after you begin cutting and cut out the wrong section...I speak from experience! (Fig. 4)

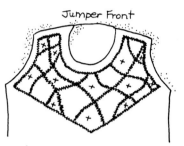

Jumper Front

X's mark sections to cut out

Fig. 4

9. Carefully pull apart the two layers and snip with the scissors into the top layer only. Cut carefully within the section and close to the stitching lines to remove the denim. For a more ragged, rugged look, you may prefer to leave a wider denim strip inside the stitching line that will eventually ravel.

This simple cutwork technique works well on a sturdy base of denim. With laundering and wear, the denim edges may change and slightly fray, but won't fall apart. For more possibilities, experiment with contrasting thread colors and more than one layer of fabric.

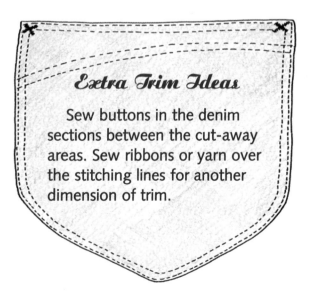

Extra Trim Ideas

Sew buttons in the denim sections between the cut-away areas. Sew ribbons or yarn over the stitching lines for another dimension of trim.

Creative Couching with a Trim Collection

Select an assortment of yarns, ribbons, decorative braids, and cord for a novel couching project on denim. Blend the trim colors with the blue of the garment for tone-on-tone decoration, or go for a bright contrast as I did with some of the trims sewn on the vest pictured. The collection of trims are wrapped and gathered together near the shoulder line and swirl away to show on both the back and front of the vest. My sister Becky is wearing this vest in our family photo on page 4.

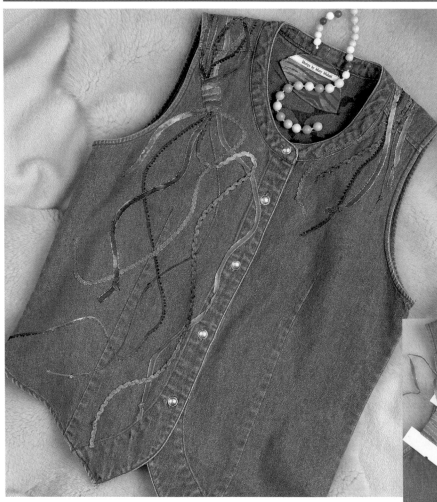

Supplies to Gather:

Denim vest

5 or 6 strips of trims, each 1-1/2 yds. long in varying widths and colors

(1) 12" trim strip, preferably a ribbon

Scrap of fabric, 2" square

Clear nylon thread for top thread

Bobbin thread

1/2 yd. tear-away stabilizer

Chalk marker

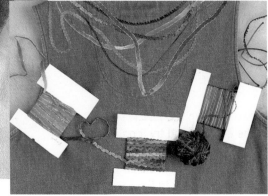

Creative Couching on a Vest

Variegated ribbons and unusual cords create the flowing lines of trim on this denim vest. Notice the pop beads at the vest neckline. They're added for my sister Becky who modeled the vest in our family picture. She received pop beads as a gift for her fifth birthday and the rest of us were so envious. We still call her the Pop Bead Queen.

Creative Couching - Vest Back

The yarns and cords extend from the front to the vest back. Some of the cards of trim I used are also shown. Remember to press the trims flat (to eliminate the bends and folds from storage on a card) before sewing them to a garment. The vest trims are from The Yarn Collection (see Resources).

Steps to Take:

1. After selecting pieces of trim, press each one to remove wrinkles or folds. If the trims are wound around a card, the foldlines may take more time to iron flat. It is always easier to remove foldlines before you sew the trims to the garment.

2. On a small piece of thin fabric, pin all the trims side by side at approximately the center of each strip of trim. Rather than making all trims the same length at each end, vary the lengths for added interest to the design, a detail you will see in the vest photo. Straight stitch or zigzag across all the trims to anchor them to the fabric. Trim away the excess fabric (Fig. 1a) and wind and pin the 12" trim strip around the anchored strips. (Fig. 1b)

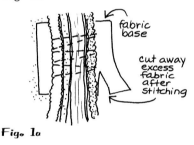

fabric base

cut away excess fabric after stitching

Fig. 1a

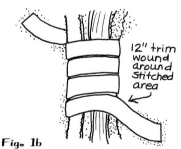

12" trim wound around stitched area

Fig. 1b

3. Place and pin the wound section on the garment and try it on to test the position. All the strips will extend from this center point either to the front of the vest or to the back of the vest and all the way around to the opposite front. Pin stabilizer to the wrong side of the garment in the areas where you plan to stitch the trims. (Fig. 2)

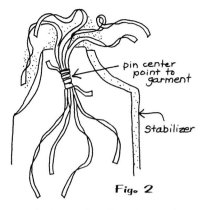

pin center point to garment

Stabilizer

Fig. 2

4. With clear nylon thread, straight stitch only the gathered and wound trim area to the garment. (Fig. 3)

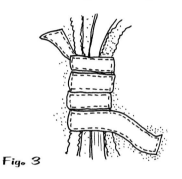

Fig. 3

5. With a chalk marker, draw swirling lines for each of the trims extending down on the garment. Use the vest pictured as a guide for your lines or draw your own swirl arrangement. I drew and stitched on the front of the vest first, then marked and sewed the trims to the back and other front of the vest. This way, the chalk markings were visible when I was ready to sew each area and didn't rub off during handling.

6. Now it's time to do the couching - sewing on top of the trim strips to attach them to the garment. From the wound gathering point, sew each strip to the garment by placing the strip over a line drawn on the garment and stitching. Some trims may overlap others, so be sure to sew down the trims underneath first. Use your choice of straight, zigzag, or triple zigzag stitches to anchor the trims. At the ends of the strips you can add a knot, turn under the raw

edge of the trim, or zigzag the ends to secure them and prevent them from raveling. (Fig. 4)

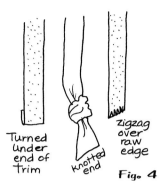

Turned under end of trim

knotted end

zigzag over raw edge

Fig. 4

7. After the stitching is complete, remove the stabilizer from the back of the garment.

8. Change the buttons on the vest if they're ordinary. I chose gold buttons to coordinate with the golden tones of the couched trims.

For another dimension to the couching, try sewing a basting stitch down the center of ribbon type trims, then pulling the thread to gather them so the edges are not flat. It's amazing how simple strips of decorative trim can add new life to a plain denim vest or shirt.

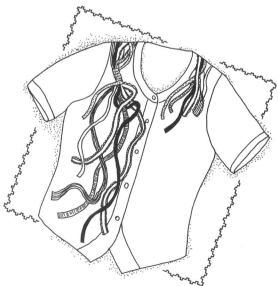

Between the Pintucks

Showcase decorative stitches, yarn, and double needle stitching between the tucks of a ready-to-wear shirt or tuxedo shirt. If your shirt doesn't have pintucks, use the same decorating techniques by drawing lines on a plain shirt front.

Decorating Between the Pintucks

Trim the channels between the shirt pintucks with a combination of interesting yarns and decorative stitching. Then add strips of trim to the collar and cuffs and change the buttons. The shirt is by Sunbelt and the yarn trims are by Sally Houk Exclusives (see Resources).

Supplies to Gather:

Denim shirt with pintucks or plain front

Yarns and trim for couching

Rayon thread for decorative stitching

Denim double needle (4.0) or other double needle (2.5 or 3.0)

Clear nylon thread

Chalk marker

Test fabric of the same color as the shirt

Optional: Lightweight stabilizer or water-soluble stabilizer

Steps to Take:

1. Prepare a plain shirt front by drawing stitching lines with a yardstick and a chalk marker. Mark and stitch only one shirt front at a time. Mark the second front just before you're ready to stitch, so the lines are fresh and easy to see. If you're drawing your own lines instead of working between pintucks, you don't even have to make them straight. Gently curved lines will still be easy to stitch and trim.

2. Depending on the weight of the denim shirt, you may need to add stabilizer to the wrong side of the garment. Start off with a trial row of stitching or couching and if the denim is too soft and the stitches don't lie flat, add stabilizer to the entire half of the shirt front you're working on.

3. Begin with couching - the process of laying on yarns, decorative trim, or cord and zigzag stitching on them to secure them to the garment. It's fun to use a variety of yarns and flat trims. Use clear nylon thread in the machine so the stitching lines are not visible. At the bottom and top of the stitching, secure the ends by zigzagging back and forth and then cut away the trim beyond the stitching. (Fig. 1) This is easier than trying to turn edges under unless the trim is a flat ribbon.

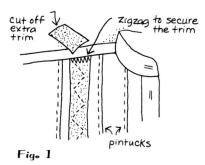

Fig. 1

4. Couch yarns between the pintucks, leaving a few rows empty for decorative stitching.

5. In some of the empty rows, sew decorative stitches, using rayon threads to contrast with the denim shirt color. Test the stitching on denim scraps the color of the shirt to determine if the thread color will be visible. (Fig. 2)

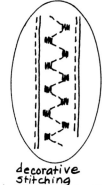

Fig. 2 decorative stitching between pintucks

6. Next, use a double needle on the machine. A denim double needle in size 4.0 handles thick denim fabrics easily. You may find that the swing of the needles in decorative stitching catches and flattens the pintucks. If you don't like that effect, use a double needle with a smaller space between the needles (2.5 or 3.0). Try two different colors of rayon thread in the double needles for an interesting effect. Test straight and decorative stitches on a scrap of denim fabric the same color as the garment. Not all thread colors will show distinctly on denim. If you select decorative stitches, try the simpler ones such as feather stitching or blanket stitching. (Fig. 3) If you have a double needle safety button on your sewing machine, activate it to prevent breaking the double needle. Experiment with different stitches to see how they change when they're made with the double needle and bordered by pintucks.

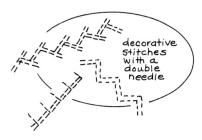

decorative stitches with a double needle

Fig. 3

7. Trim the collar and cuffs with one or more rows of flat ribbon couched in place with a decorative double needle stitch using contrasting color threads. (Fig. 4) On these areas, you will not need stabilizer since you are stitching through more than one layer of denim. I removed the cuff buttons before stitching since I planned to change them anyway.

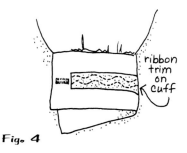

ribbon trim on cuff

Fig. 4

8. Now that your shirt is magnificent with its extra trim, change the buttons. Though it's a small detail, it's always worth it and adds even more class to your pintucked shirt.

Thread Colors on Denim

From my experiments, medium and dark tone threads blend with denim and are hard to see. Light and very bright colors show up best when you want the stitching to stand out. Also try neon, light-sensitive, and flat metallic (such as Sulky Sliver) threads for contrast on denim fabrics.

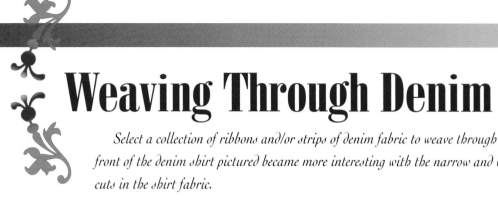

Weaving Through Denim

Select a collection of ribbons and/or strips of denim fabric to weave through a garment. The plain front of the denim shirt pictured became more interesting with the narrow and wide strips woven through cuts in the shirt fabric.

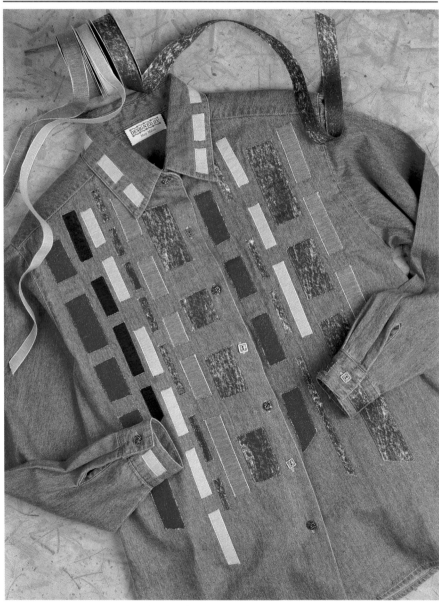

Ribbons Woven Through Denim

A selection of ribbons by C.M. Offray & Sons winds through cuts in the front, collar, and cuffs of this denim shirt. Each cuff has different ribbon trim, just for fun. I chose two shapes of gold buttons to replace the original, ordinary shirt buttons.

Supplies to Gather:

Denim shirt with plain front

6 ribbons or cut strips of fabric - 1 yard will usually be enough for two strips of weaving

Double stick fusible bonding web: Steam A Seam 2 or AppliqEase

1 yd. lightweight tricot knit fusible interfacing

Nylon invisible thread - either clear or smoke, depending on the ribbon colors

Bodkin

Chalk marker

Steps to Take:

1. With the denim garment on a table, plan the number of ribbon trims and the ribbon arrangement. Pull out the wires in any wire-edge ribbons. Cut strips of double stick fusible bonding web and apply it to the back of each ribbon. Remove the paper backing so the ribbons can temporarily adhere to the garment for marking their placement.

2. With a chalk marker, mark both long sides of each ribbon. (Fig. 1)

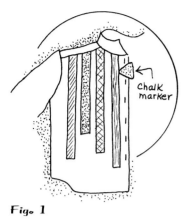

Fig. 1

Check to see that the shirt's placket facings are out of the way of the weaving lines. Pin them away, if necessary. Remove the strips, one at a time, and mark and cut the horizontal lines for weaving between the two chalk lines. (Fig. 2)

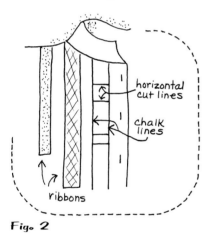

Fig. 2

I chose to weave in and out at irregular intervals so the weaving lines don't line up horizontally. Cut carefully with a rotary cutter and a mat underneath or use scissors, making sure to cut only between the vertical chalk lines.

3. With a bodkin on one end of the ribbon, lace the ribbon strip through the cut lines. At the bottom of the strip, turn the edge of the ribbon under if you want a nonraveling edge. Adjust the strip in the garment so it lies flat. Continue to mark, cut, and weave the other strips through the garment.

Weaving Ribbon with a Bodkin

Fold up the end of the ribbon and lock the bodkin gripper teeth on the doubled ribbon. Then weave the bodkin and ribbon through the cuts in the garment.

4. Use pinking shears to cut a piece of lightweight interfacing to cover the entire woven area on the wrong side of the garment under the weaving. The pinked edges will prevent any shadowing of the interfacing on the right side of the garment. (Fig. 3) Fuse the interfacing in place, making sure the ribbon strips are all lying flat within the woven lines.

Fig. 3

5. Now it's time to sew the ribbons in place. With a narrow zigzag stitch and clear nylon top thread, sew down and across the ribbons and cut lines on the right side of the garment, then sew back up to catch the other side of the ribbon. (Fig. 4) Cut off any loose threads of denim. The interfacing on the back will help stabilize the stitching so you won't need a separate stabilizer unless the garment fabric is very soft.

Fig. 4

6. The same weaving was added to the collar and cuffs of the pictured shirt but instead of cutting through both layers of the collar and cuffs, I used scissors to cut through only the top layers of fabric so no interfacing was needed. Use bobbin thread to match the garment color for both the collar and cuffs.

7. To add another classy detail to the garment, change the buttons.

You can create a one-of-a-kind denim garment as you weave ribbons through the garment fabric. A plain front with no pockets or other details is the easiest to weave through, but weaving ribbons through the garment's "obstructions" could provide a creative challenge!

Sashiko Style Topstitching

Use quilting templates as an easy guide to follow for stitching on denim. To simulate the look of Japanese sashiko quilting, machine stitch with YLI Jeans Thread - a substantial thread developed for use on denim - and a topstitching needle.

Denim Dress with Sashiko Style Topstitching

It was easy to pin and sew around a paper quilting stencil from W.E. Wright Co. to the top front and skirt of this dress. The thread I used, Jeans Thread by YLI, matched the topstitching already on the dress.

Sashiko Stitching Experiments

A variety of shades of denim fabric and Jeans Thread were chosen for experiments with decorative stitching. Quilting templates to trace through or pin on provide easy stitching guides. The paper stencil is a Stitchable Stencil by Hari Walner for W. E. Wrights.

Supplies to Gather:

Denim dress with plain front

Jeans Thread by YLI

Standard thread for the bobbin

Topstitching needle - size 90 or 100

1/2 yd. lightweight tear-away or lightweight cut-away stabilizer

Fabric and stabilizer for practice

Quilting template

Chalk marker

Steps to Take:

1. With the special thread and needle required for this project, it is advisable to experiment before beginning your project on a garment. On denim practice fabric, secure the stabilizer to the back with pins or fusible spray. Try both the tear-away and cut-away stabilizer to see which works best for you. If the tear-away variety loosens or distorts stitches when it is removed, you may prefer to use a soft, cut-away stabilizer that remains on the garment and supports the stitching or can be removed by cutting.

2. Start with a topstitching needle and Jeans Thread on the machine and standard sewing thread in the bobbin. You can use matching threads or use a shade of blue thread in the bobbin to blend with the denim.

3. Begin sewing slowly. Loosen the top tension slightly. Sew with a straight stitch to practice for this project and try different stitch lengths. I chose a 2.5 length for the dress shown. After a few rows of test

stitching, you may want to chalk mark a portion of the quilting template to practice guiding your stitches around the curves and angles. After you've completed your practice, try removing the tear-away stabilizer on the back of the fabric. This test will help determine which type of stabilizer to use on the garment.

4. When you're ready to begin on a garment, add the stabilizer to the wrong side of the area where you plan to stitch. If there are facings or plackets on the garment that could get caught in the stitching, pin them out of the way.

5. Mark or pin on the quilting template. I used pin-on Stitchable Stencils from W.E. Wright. (Fig. 1)

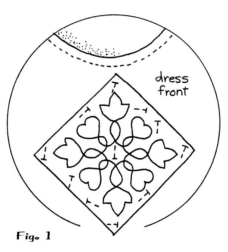

dress front

Fig. 1

Continuous stitching quilting templates allow you to start sewing at any spot and sew all the way around without stopping, where other templates require frequent starting and stopping. Make sure the lines are easy to see and that the chalk marks don't rub off before you get the garment to the sewing machine. If you plan to sew in more than one area, mark only one section at a time and finish sewing before marking another section.

6. As with the practice stitching, sew slowly as you guide the fabric and design lines to the needle. After the sewing is completed, pull the top threads to the back of the garment and knot them securely. Remove any tear-away stabilizer or cut and trim nontearing stabilizer.

The dress featured in the photograph has sashiko topstitching on the bottom of the skirt using half of the motif shown on the dress top. Other good places for the stitching include the back of a garment, cuffs, or a hemline border. Jeans Thread is available in many colors to blend or contrast with many shades of denim or chambray. See the shirt on page 102 for another way to use Jeans Thread with decorative stitches.

A portion of the quilting stencil is repeated near the hemline of the dress.

Denim Blazer with Style

Shiny trims, elegant fabrics, and new buttons turn an ordinary denim blazer into evening wear. Now you can be comfortable and glamorous at the same time!

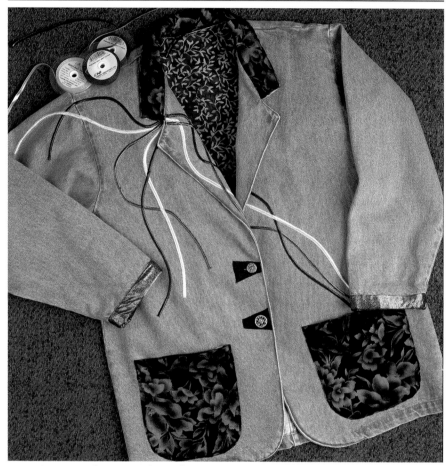

Denim Blazer with Style

Metallic bias trim, elegant fabric covers for the collar, pockets, and cuffs, and new shiny buttons turn a plain blazer into a special occasion garment. The blazer is by Sunbelt (see Resources).

Supplies to Gather:

Denim blazer

Fabrics for covering collar, pockets, and cuffs

Metallic fusible bias tape - assorted colors and lengths

Replacement buttons

Denim needle

6.0 double needle

Small pieces of nonfray fabric, such as Ultrasuede, to cover buttonholes and button areas

2 spools clear nylon thread and threads to match fabrics

Paper-backed fusible web or fusible spray

Chalk marker or wash-away marking pen

Steps to Take:

1. Use the pattern making directions in the Workshop section on page 121 to make a collar pattern and a pattern for the lower pockets. If you'd like to cover the jacket lapels with fabric, make a pattern from the lapels. Add 1/2" seam allowances to the collar or lapel pattern and 3/4" seam allowances to the pocket pattern.

2. Cut two pocket patterns from fabric. Turn under 1/4" on the sides and 1/2" on the top edges to make the pocket covers larger than the original pockets so they are easier to sew on, beyond the thick seams of the original pockets. Pin the pocket covers over the original pockets, lining up the top edges with the pocket opening. With the denim needle on the machine, sew across the top edge to secure the cover to the original pocket, making the pocket still usable. (Fig. 1) Sew around the sides and bottom edges.

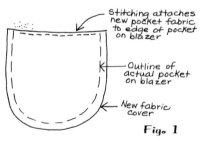

3. Pin the collar fabric right side out to the original collar, turn under the edges, and sew in place. (Fig. 2)

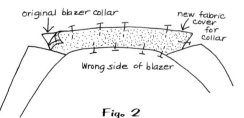

4. To change the buttons, remove the original riveted buttons by cutting through the denim one layer at a time very close to the riveted button. Refer to page 122 of the Workshop section. Wrap a piece of nonfray fabric over the edge of the jacket so it covers the holes on the front and back. Sew the fabric to the jacket, then sew on new buttons (refer to the photo).

Riveted Button Replacement

With a sharp scissors, cut off the blazer's original riveted buttons. Wrap and sew fabric around the front and back of the area to cover the hole. Then sew on a shiny silver button to add a touch of style to the jacket.

5. To add style to the buttonholes, cover them with pieces of nonfray fabric on the front of the jacket. Make sure the fabric piece is longer than the original buttonhole in the jacket. Use paper-backed fusible web or fusible spray on the wrong side of the fabric pieces to secure them to the jacket for sewing. Zigzag the edges with matching or clear thread. From the wrong side of the jacket front, cut a buttonhole in the nonfray fabric by going through the existing buttonhole. You may want to first sew around the buttonholes with a narrow zigzag, then cut the buttonholes open. (Fig. 3)

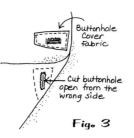

Buttonhole Cover Fabric

Cut buttonhole open from the wrong side.

Fig. 3

6. Now let's cover the sleeve cuffs so they can be rolled up to show off an elegant fabric. Turn the sleeve inside out and use the sleeve end as a pattern. Most jacket sleeves will be tapered toward the bottom. Place the sleeve on a piece of folded fabric and cut the new cuff 7" long and the width of the sleeve plus 1/2" for seam allowances. With right sides together, sew the side seams of each cuff with a 1/4" seam allowance. Serge or turn under the top or wider edge of the cuff fabric and press it. Line up the right side of the cuff seam to the right side of the jacket seam and pin the cuff in place 1" up from the sleeve end. Sew around the unfinished edge of the cuff fabric. (Fig. 4)

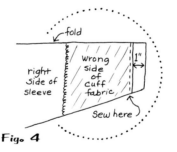

fold

right Side of sleeve

Wrong Side of Cuff fabric

1"

Sew here

Fig. 4

Fold the fabric over the sleeve end and smooth and pin it inside the sleeve. Sew the top edge to the sleeve, making sure the bobbin thread matches the denim fabric. (Fig. 5)

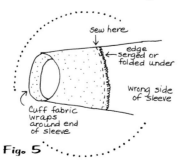

Sew here

edge serged or folded under

wrong side of sleeve

Cuff fabric wraps around end of sleeve

Fig. 5

7. The final addition is metallic fusible bias tape. I used three colors on the jacket. Using the photo as a guide,

draw curving lines on the jacket front, lapel, and opposite side with a chalk marker or wash-away marking pen. Try the jacket on to test the line locations. On the jacket sides and sleeves, the lines can become distorted by the folds that form when the jacket is on a body, so the line locations are worth checking. Fuse one strip of metallic bias tape along the first line you plan to stitch and add a few pins for extra security. (Fig. 6) You will cross the first strip with the subsequent bias strips you sew to the jacket.

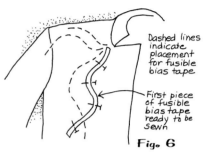

Dashed lines indicate placement for fusible bias tape

First piece of fusible bias tape ready to be sewn

Fig. 6

8. Set up your sewing machine with the 6.0 double needle and two spools of clear thread. On a scrap of fabric, fuse a small section of metallic bias tape for practice. Stitch the tape to the fabric with a narrow zigzag stitch to catch both sides of the bias in one sewing. If your machine has a double needle safety button, activate it before stitching.

9. Sew the first piece of bias to the jacket. Turn under the raw edges at the ends of the strips before sewing. (Fig. 7) Continue to fuse and sew additional strips of bias on the lines you drew on the jacket and the lapels.

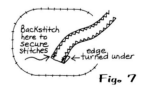

Backstitch here to secure stitches

edge turned under

Fig. 7

Make it a personal challenge to decorate a denim jacket suitable for evening wear. Choose sequins, lamé fabrics, glittery appliques or the trims shown on this jacket. Consider the embellishment ideas on this jacket as stepping stones to your own inspirations.

New Twists on Seminole Patchwork

When you and I first learned to make Seminole patchwork, we followed strict rules and very careful measurements for precise work. Now I'm asking you to set aside the rules and try some new versions of this patchwork. Try these three creative effects and give new life to spare fabric strips and pieces. See what you think.

Denim Shirt with Wavy Edge Seminole Patchwork and Ultrasuede Rickrack

With nontraditional Seminole patchwork yokes and curvy strips of Ultrasuede, this shirt gets a stylish make-over. Wavy strips of Hoffman cotton fabrics are sewn together with decorative yarn over the edges. Cut sections of the panel created with the strips are sewn together and then turned into yoke fronts for the shirt. Wrapping strips of Ultrasuede around the collar and cuffs adds additional color and durability to the shirt.

Supplies to Gather:

Denim shirt

Selection of 45" wide fabrics for cutting narrow (3" or less) strips across the fabric grain

Thread to blend with colors of fabric

Rotary cutter

Cutting mat

Ruler

1/2 yd. tear-away stabilizer

1/2 yd. lightweight fusible interfacing

Fusible spray

Optional: Yarn for couching

WAVY EDGE SEMINOLE WITH COUCHING

Varying the fabric strip widths creates an exciting "movement" in Seminole patchwork piecing. Wavy Edge Seminole can be used to create a pocket, to cover a collar, or to highlight the yokes of a denim shirt, as described in the following instructions. Adjust steps 6 and 7 to accommodate your specific project.

Steps to Take:

1. Measure the area to be covered with Wavy Edge Seminole, for example the shirt yokes pictured. Add 8" to the length and 2" to the width to calculate the number of fabric strips needed for piecing and restitching.

2. Using several fabrics, cut fabric strips with one wavy edge and one straight edge. On the top fabric only, cut straight edges and allow for extra fabric on both the top and bottom strips. For the shirt yoke pictured, I used five different fabrics. (Fig. 1)

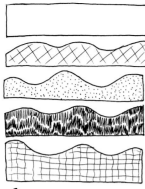

Fig. 1

3. Arrange the strips on a piece of stabilizer. Spray the wrong side of each strip with fusible spray and place them in order from top to bottom, making sure each strip overlaps the previous one.

4. Using clear nylon thread or thread to match the fabrics, zigzag over the wavy edges of the strips. If desired, add yarn or thin cording over the edge and zigzag over it again or stitch with a decorative stitch and thread to couch the yarn in place. (Fig. 2)

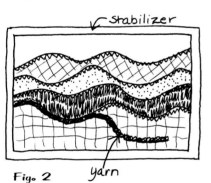

Fig. 2

5. Remove the stabilizer from the back. Cut the band of fabrics into pieces of different widths. Arrange the pieces by alternating the top and bottom edges as shown. Sew the pieces with right sides together and a 1/4" seam allowance. (Fig. 3)

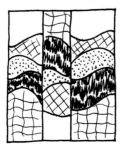

Fig. 3

6. Make tracing paper patterns for the yokes, following the Workshop instructions for pattern making on page 121. Cut the yoke shape plus a 1/2" seam allowance all the way around from the center of a piece of paper so it forms a "window." (Fig. 4a) Position the paper window on the patchwork piece to determine where you want to cut the yoke pieces, then trace the shape onto the patchwork. Cut out the two yoke pieces in this way. (Fig. 4b)

Fig. 4a

window placed over pieced fabric

Fig. 4b

7. Pin the centers of the patchwork yokes to the shirt fronts right side up. Turn under and pin the edges to meet the seamlines at the shoulder, arm, neckline, and front plackets. (Fig. 5) Sew the yokes to the shirt around the yoke edges with clear thread and a narrow zigzag so the stitching is nearly invisible.

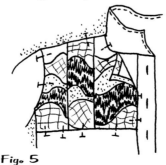

Fig. 5

ULTRASUEDE RICKRACK WRAP

Other details on the shirt include a change of buttons and Ultrasuede Rickrack. Cut strips of Ultrasuede with a wavy edge rotary cutter and turn it into stylish rickrack for the edge of a collar and cuffs. It preserves the collar and cuff edges and washes with ease.

Supplies to Gather:

Shirt with collar and cuffs

1/8 yd. Ultrasuede or a 9" x 12" piece

Fusible spray

Clear nylon thread or thread to match Ultrasuede

Rotary cutter with scallop edge

Ruler

Cutting board

Steps to Take:

1. Measure the collar and cuff edges and cut strips of Ultrasuede with a scallop edge and a straight edge. The strips should measure 1" in width from the top of the scallops to the straight edge. (Fig. 1)

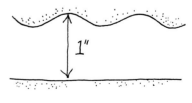

1"

Fig. 1

2. With wrong sides together, fold the strips in half lengthwise with the scallop edge meeting the straight edge. Place a press cloth over the top and press. (Fig. 2)

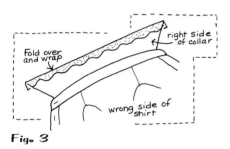

Press cloth over Ultrasuede for pressing

Right side of fabric

Fig. 2

3. Open the fold and spray the wrong side of the fabric with fusible spray. Wrap the long straight edge of the collar first. (Fig. 3)

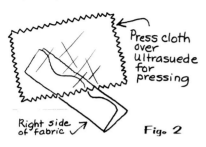

right side of collar

Fold over and wrap

wrong side of shirt

Fig. 3

Position and finger press the scallop edge onto the right side of the collar with the fold at the collar edge and the straight edge on the underside of the collar. If you had to piece the Ultrasuede to cover the collar edge, meet or overlap the ends.

4. Fill the bobbin with thread to match the Ultrasuede and use clear nylon or matching color thread as the top thread. Sew on the right side of the Ultrasuede with either a straight stitch along the scallop edge or with a blanket stitch for a more invisible attachment. Wrap and sew the shorter collar ends and trim the Ultrasuede where the collar lines meet. (Fig. 4)

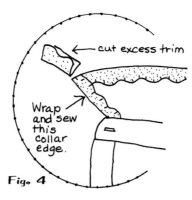

cut excess trim

Wrap and sew this collar edge.

Fig. 4

5. Use the same procedure to prepare the Ultrasuede strips for the cuffs. Wrap and sew the edges with either a straight stitch or blanket stitch. Trim the ends of the Ultrasuede to meet the cuff ends.

Other nonfraying fabrics such as faux suede, Ultraleather, or vinyl could be chosen for this rickrack wrap. It's an easy and elegant way to cover shirt edges that may be worn, stained, or in need of durable, stylish trim.

VARIATION #1 - DENIM SEMINOLE

Denim Seminole Patchwork

This new Seminole technique produces a unique panel of pieced fabrics for garment accents on collars, cuffs, pocket covers, or to use as appliques. See the strips of fusible interfacing on the wrong side of the panel.

This Seminole method works well with thick fabrics because there are no bulky seam allowances to cause problems. All fabric edges are butted together rather than overlapped. Denim is a good candidate for this technique as are corduroy, Ultrasuede, canvas, and others.

1. Cut strips from different shades and colors of denim. Use the wrong side of denim for lighter shades.

2. Cut 1/2" strips of lightweight fusible interfacing. Gray or black is a good color choice for interfacing when working with denims.

3. Place the right side of the strips down, with adjoining edges meeting, and fuse a strip of interfacing over the top of the butting edges. Do this fusing carefully so edges meet precisely under the interfacing. (Fig. 1)

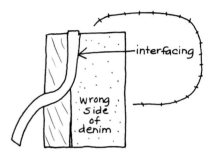

interfacing

wrong side of denim

Fig. 1

4. With smoke colored nylon thread, zigzag on the right side of the fabrics, making sure the zigzag is wide enough to catch both sides of the denim strips and secure them to the interfacing. (Fig. 2)

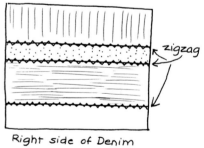

zigzag

Right side of Denim

Fig. 2

5. Cut pieces of the denim band of fabric. The pieces can vary in width. Plan the arrangement of the pieces by alternating the top and bottom edges. (Fig. 3)

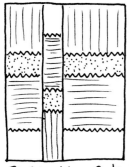

Right side of denim

Fig. 3

6. With more 1/2" strips of fusible interfacing, fuse the butted edges of the pieces together on the wrong sides, then sew again on the right side with the zigzag stitch wide enough to catch both sides. (Fig. 4)

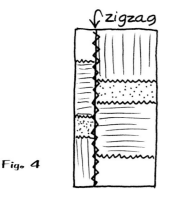

↓ zigzag

Fig. 4

You have created a piece of patchwork to decorate part of a garment, to make a pocket or yoke section. Appliques could also be cut from the denim Seminole piece.

VARIATION #2 - WEDGE SEMINOLE

Wedge Seminole Patchwork
Experiment with wedge shapes for a different look.

Instead of cutting fabric strips a consistent width, cut wedge shapes with one end of the strip wide and the opposite end narrow, but at least 1" wide. Cut the first strip and use it as a pattern for the other strips. Use an even number of strips for this technique and make sure both the right and left sides of the band of fabrics you sew together are the same vertical height.

Steps to Take:

1. Plan the strip arrangement by aligning a wide end to a narrow end. With right sides together, use a 1/4" seam allowance to sew the strips together. Press all the seam allowances in one direction. (Fig. 1)

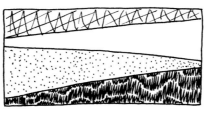

Fig. 1

2. Cut wedge sections alternately and one at a time from each end of the strip and arrange them by alternating top and bottom edges. (Fig. 2) With right sides together, sew the pieces together using a 1/4" seam allowance.

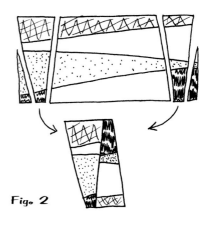

Fig. 2

Experiment with this method and use it for trimming a portion of a garment. See the top basket on the jacket on page 49 for an example of Wedge Seminole as the cover for a pocket.

From Pieces to Projects

Wavy Edge, Denim Seminole, and Wedge Seminole piecing can provide inspiration for countless garment decorations. Think pockets, cuffs, belts, yokes, and more. Measure the area to be decorated first and plan the piecing to use slightly more fabric in both directions. The strips you cut and sew can then be proportional and color coordinated with your garment.

In the mood to experiment without a specific project in mind? Cut and sew strips to create pieced yardage, then decide later on the best use for your original piecework.

part **2**

DENIM ON DENIM

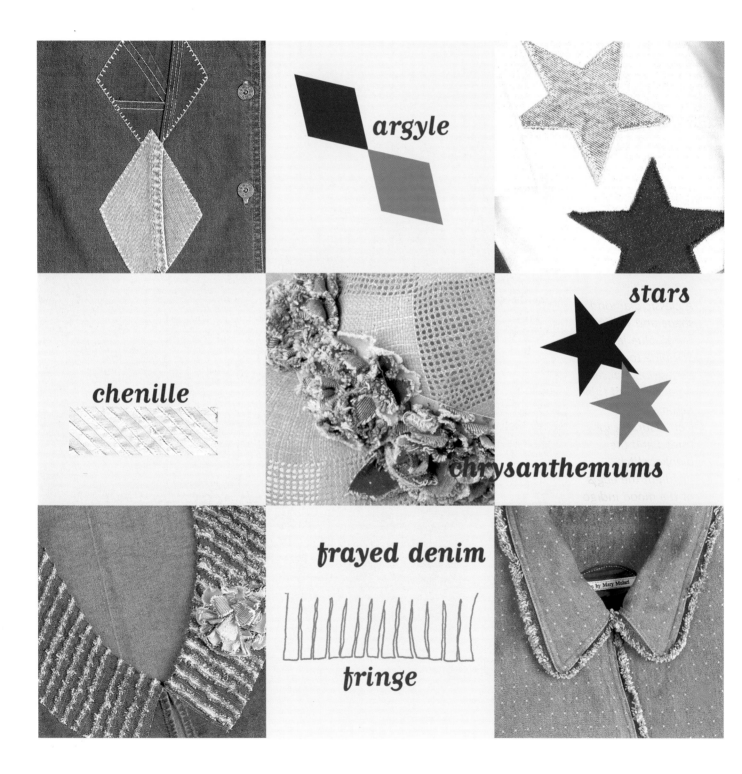

argyle

stars

chenille

chrysanthemums

frayed denim

fringe

Mood Indigo Argyles

You'll recognize sections of blue jeans in the diamond shapes sewn to the front of this denim shirt. I used parts cut from three different pairs of jeans to feature different color tones, stitching, and seam patterns.

Mood Indigo Argyles Shirt

A classic diamond shape and sections of old blue jeans combine to produce dimensional accents on one side of this denim shirt. Contrasting color thread and the blanket stitch highlight the edges of the mood indigo argyles.

Supplies to Gather:

Denim shirt with plain front

Old blue jeans to cut up

Denim sewing machine needle

Jeans Thread for applique stitching

1/4 yd. stabilizer

Fusible spray

Chalk marker

Steps to Take:

1. Trace the argyle pattern. Cut the pattern from a larger piece of paper to make a window to view the details of the shape. (Fig. 1) Use a chalk marker to outline each of the five argyles on the jeans and cut them out. Try to avoid placing a thick seam at the top or bottom points of the diamonds as these areas will overlap other diamonds if you follow the design pattern shown on the shirt pictured.

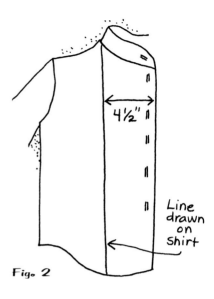

Fig. 2

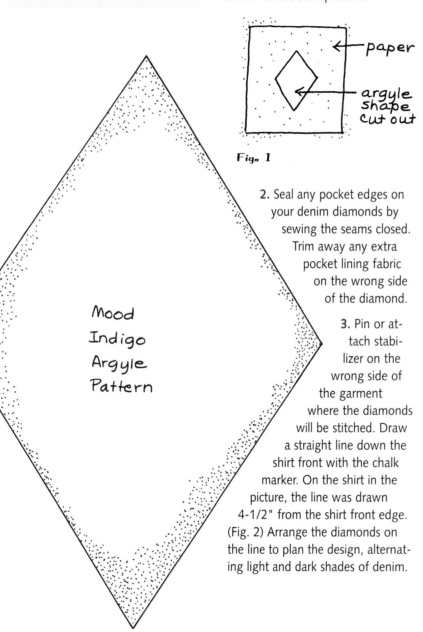

paper

argyle shape cut out

Fig. 1

Mood Indigo Argyle Pattern

2. Seal any pocket edges on your denim diamonds by sewing the seams closed. Trim away any extra pocket lining fabric on the wrong side of the diamond.

3. Pin or attach stabilizer on the wrong side of the garment where the diamonds will be stitched. Draw a straight line down the shirt front with the chalk marker. On the shirt in the picture, the line was drawn 4-1/2" from the shirt front edge. (Fig. 2) Arrange the diamonds on the line to plan the design, alternating light and dark shades of denim.

4. Use a denim needle on the sewing machine to ease sewing through several thick denim areas on the diamonds. I chose to sew the diamonds on the shirt with a blanket stitch and light colored Jeans Thread so the stitching would create obvious contrast on each diamond. As with all Jeans Thread/denim needle projects, expect to loosen the top tension slightly and sew slowly and carefully, particularly over thick areas of fabric and stitching. Experiment first on scraps of fabric if you haven't tried this thread or needle before.

5. After the stitching is completed, pull the thread tails to the back of the garment and knot them. Remove the stabilizer.

6. Remove the regular buttons and replace them with silver buttons to blend with the denim shirt color.

Think of how interesting these argyle diamonds would look on a sweatshirt, vest, or just about anything that needs decorating. You'll never look at jeans seamlines again without thinking about how they'd appear in an argyle shape.

Scattered Stars – A Project by Luveta Nickels

Let's go shopping! I was searching for that perfect denim garment in a different color to decorate with old blue jeans parts. After picking up supplies for my husband at a local farm store, I checked out the men's department with its utility work clothing. I was delighted to find this cream colored denim jacket on a closeout. I always love a bargain and now make the farm store a regular stop on my shopping excursions.

The "new and improved" OshKosh jacket features a zipper placket cover made from the flat-felled side seam of jeans and decorations of leftover pockets, waistbands, and belt loops. Bias cut fabric adds extra color along the jacket seams. Star appliques are cut from contrasting shades of denim. You'll also see watch pockets and broken zippers, metal star nail heads, and red snaps.

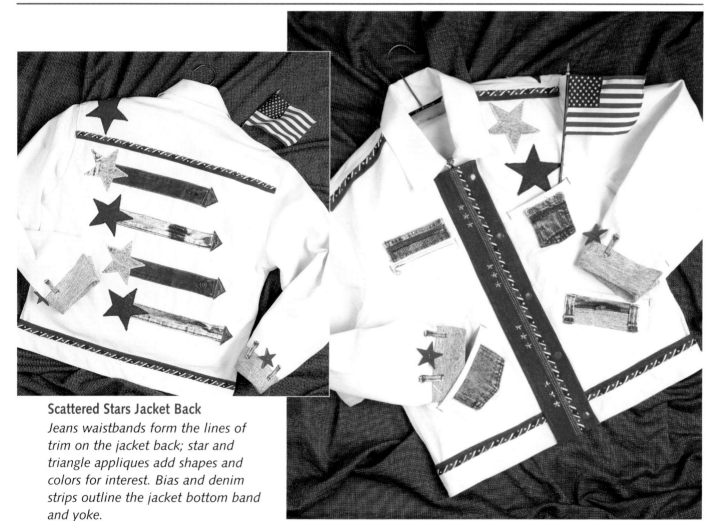

Scattered Stars Jacket Back

Jeans waistbands form the lines of trim on the jacket back; star and triangle appliques add shapes and colors for interest. Bias and denim strips outline the jacket bottom band and yoke.

Scattered Stars Jacket

Pieces of old blue jeans star in their role as trim for a work jacket with a patriotic theme. You'll recognize jeans belt loops, pockets, and a zipper in their new use as decorations.

Scattered
Stars
Patterns

Supplies to Gather:

Denim jacket with zipper front

2 old pairs adult size jeans in contrasting denim shades

1/2 yd. small print fabric

1/2 yd. heavy fusible interfacing

1/2 yd. fusible web

1 yd. tear-away stabilizer

Scraps of Lamé Leather

20 decorative star-shaped nail heads

5 red snaps (lg. prong size 20)

2 large decorative star buttons for cuff trim

Rotary Cutter

Cutting mat

Ruler

Utility razor knife or Olfa Rotary Point Cutter

Pliers

Pencil eraser

Kitchen teaspoon

Stiff old toothbrush

Snap setting tool

Jean-A-Ma-Jig

Space-Tape to mark evenly spaced buttonholes or snaps

Schmetz denim needle - size 80/12

Work Jacket Ready for a Make-Over
Begin Luveta Nickel's denim jacket project with an ordinary jacket like this one she found in the men's department of a local farm supply store.

Steps to Take:

Prepare and Cut the Blue Jeans

1. Wash the blue jeans so the fabric is fresh, clean, and ready to cut and sew. Cut apart each pair of jeans at the inside leg seam, cutting next to the seam.

2. Remove the stitches on the front crotch seam of each pair of jeans with a utility knife or point cutter. Break the zipper and use pliers to remove the metal stop at the bottom of the zipper. Lay the jeans flat as shown. (Fig. 1) Press with very hot steam. (Pressing before you cut helps to eliminate some of the character lines and provides a flat, smooth piece of denim.)

Fig. 1

3. When removing the back pockets, I have found that using the utility knife to loosen the bar tacks and then using brute strength to tear them off the jeans works better and faster than trying to pick every stitch. Seam rippers are not strong enough or long enough to grasp for leverage. If the pockets have rivets in the corners, simply cut a hole in the jeans behind the rivet to release the rivet from the jeans and again tear it away using brute strength. Use the stiff toothbrush to brush away the original stitches left on the waistband and back pockets.

4. Cut the following pieces from the two pairs of jeans, using the illustration as a guide: (Fig.2)

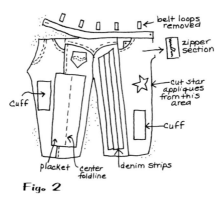

Fig. 2

* the waistband from both pairs

* 3 large light denim star appliques cut from pattern

* 4 large dark denim star appliques cut from pattern

* 2 light denim cuffs (See step 1 of "Sleeve Cuffs" on page 35)

* 1 dark denim zipper placket (See step 5 of "Decorate the Jacket Front" on page 34)

* 1-1/2" wide dark denim strips for trim. To determine how many strips you'll need, measure the length of the jacket's back yoke seam, front shoulder seams, and bottom band of the jacket and add the three measurements. Cut enough 1-1/2" wide strips to equal this total length. (It is okay to piece together strips for the bottom band, but with adult length jeans, piecing may not be necessary.)

Cut the Bias Fabric Strips

1. Cut the same number of print fabric bias strips as you cut of denim strips, 1-1/2" wide to match the 1-1/2" denim strips. Cut an extra print fabric strip to trim the front zipper cover.

Decorate the Bottom Band, Back Yoke, and Shoulder Seams

1. Press the 1-1/2" bias fabric and denim strips in half lengthwise with

wrong sides together. Place the two strips on top of one another with the print fabric on top.

2. Pin the raw edges of the strips along the jacket's bottom band seam, starting 1-1/2" from the zipper on the left side of the jacket and working around to the other side of the zipper. Turn under the raw ends of the strips so they meet the zipper seam on the right side of the jacket. With the denim needle on the machine, sew along the strips, 1/4" from the raw edges, through all the layers of fabric.

3. Fold down the print fabric only, bringing the folded edge over the raw edges of the fabric strips. Stitch down the folded edge. (Fig. 3) I left the folded edge of the denim strip loose, but you could secure it to the jacket with topstitching.

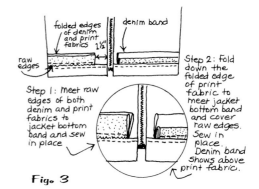

Fig. 3

4. Use this same procedure to apply the fabric strips to the back yoke and shoulder seams.

Decorate the Jacket Front

1. The construction of this jacket allowed me to remove the manufacturer's stitching along the pocket binding of both lower pockets and around the outline of the right chest pocket. I could then topstitch the jeans watch pocket to the jacket without sewing the functional pocket closed. Be careful around the

corner rivets. I used a Jean-A-Ma-Jig to level the sewing machine foot. (Fig. 4)

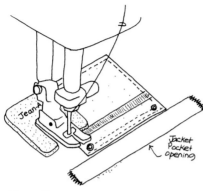

Fig. 4

If you are unable to get close enough to the rivet to sew safely, zigzag a few stitches at the top edge of the pocket to hold it in place. Then resew the chest pocket fabric back on the jacket by sewing from the wrong side of the garment so you can easily see the pocket edges. (Fig. 5)

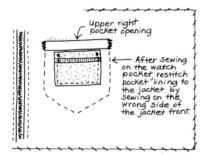

Fig. 5

2. Cut off the top third of one jeans back pocket. Stitch a strip of red Leather Lamé near the top of the cut-off section. (Fig. 6)

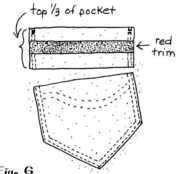

Fig. 6

Place and pin the cut edge right side down above the left chest pocket edge. Sew across, using a scant 1/8" seam. Flip the pocket flap up, press and stitch across the folded edge and up each short side to secure the decorated pocket section. (Fig. 7)

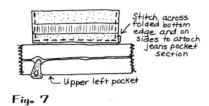

Fig. 7

3. Sew the bottom 2/3 of the jeans pocket to the lower left jacket pocket, as shown in the photograph. If possible, open the binding on the jacket pocket edge and insert the jeans pocket raw edge. (Fig. 8)

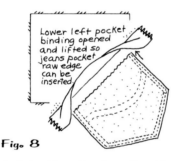

Fig. 8

4. Cut a 4" section from the side of a broken jeans zipper with the zipper pull on it. Turn under and press one of the 4" edges and slide the opposite raw edge into an opening on the jacket's lower right pocket binding. Insert two jean belt loops at each end of the zipper strip to cover the zipper ends. Sew the zipper section and belt loops to the jacket. Restitch the binding edges closed on both lower pockets. (Fig. 9)

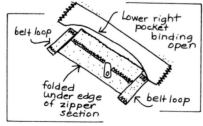

Fig. 9

5. Now you're ready to make the placket that covers the zipper. Cut the placket fabric about 1-1/2" shorter than the length of the jacket zipper. Use the flat-felled seam on one of the jeans legs as the center front guide (see Fig. 2). The width of the piece should include an equal distance on either side of the flat-felled seam and the foldline placed so you can create a self facing. For example, I cut my placket 7" wide with the foldline at 3-1/2" with the jeans seam as a visual center front. (Fig. 10)

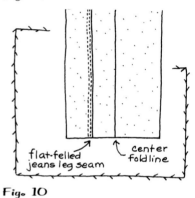

Fig. 10

6. Apply fusible interfacing to the entire wrong side of the placket piece. Sew a folded strip of bias print fabric beside the flat-felled seam as described in steps 2 and 3 of the "Decorate the Bottom Band…" instructions on page 33.

7. Push the star nail head prongs through the right side of the placket. You'll need to use the pencil eraser to finish pushing them all the way through the denim placket. Use Space-Tape to help with even spacing.

8. Use the rounded tip of a kitchen teaspoon to bend the prongs of the nail heads securely to the wrong side of the placket. Fold the placket with right sides together, stitch across both ends, turn right side out, and press. (Fig. 11)

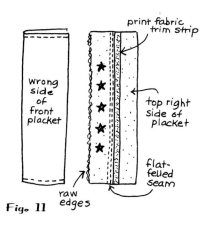

Fig. 11

(labels in Fig. 11: print fabric trim strip; wrong side of front placket; top right side of placket; flat-felled seam; raw edges)

9. Use Space-Tape to determine snap placement and apply the red snaps with a snap setting tool. This is easier than applying the snaps after the placket is attached to the jacket.

10. Lay the placket front side on the left side of jacket about 1-1/2" from the jacket zipper. Stitch a scant 1/8" seam, being sure to catch both edges of the placket on the jacket. Press towards the right front and topstitch the placket near the stitching to hold it in place. (Fig. 12)

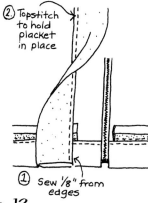

(labels in Fig. 12: ② Topstitch to hold placket in place; ① Sew 1/8" from edges)

Fig. 12

11. Apply the snap bottoms to the jacket front, carefully matching placement with the decorative snaps on the placket.

Decorate the Jacket Back

1. Mark placement lines for the waistband trim on the back of the jacket with a straight edge and a wash-away marking pen. My lines are about 2-1/4" apart and staggered by 1" Jean waistbands vary in

width so plan the placement to your liking. (Fig. 13)

(labels in Fig. 13: Back of Jacket; 2¼")

Fig. 13

2. Cut the jean waistbands in approximate 10" lengths. Open or cut away the stitching at the finished ends of the waistbands and press the ends flat. This will reduce bulk when adding the star appliques and the Lamé Leather triangles.

3. Place tear-away stabilizer on the wrong side of the jacket back, beneath the placement lines. Sew the jeans waistbands to the jacket along the top and bottom edges.

4. Cut a 2-1/2" square of Lamé Leather into four triangles as shown. (Fig. 14)

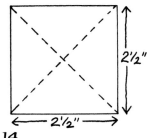

(labels in Fig. 14: 2½"; 2½")

Fig. 14

5. Sew the triangles across one of the raw ends of the waistbands using a straight stitch. Refer to the photograph of the jacket back.

6. On paper-backed fusible web, trace six large stars using the applique pattern on page 32. Fuse and cut out the traced stars from different parts of the jeans to get lighter and darker shades. Place four of the

stars on the waistband ends on the jacket back, and two stars on the upper right front of the jacket, placing stabilizer on the wrong side of the jacket beneath the area for sewing. Use a traditional satin stitch or another variety of satin stitching to sew around the stars. I found the shading stitch, with its irregular edge, covered the star points better. (Fig. 15)

(label in Fig. 15: Shading stitch on star appliques)

Fig. 15

7. After stitching the stars, remove the stabilizer from the back and front of the wrong side of the jacket.

Add New Sleeve Cuffs

1. Measure around the jacket sleeves and cut new 4" wide cuffs from the jeans. Serge or clean finish one of the raw edges of the denim on each cuff. Press under 1/4" on the serged edge.

2. Line up the unfinished long edge of each cuff so the right side of the denim is even with the wrong side of the sleeve edge. Stitch around the sleeve. (Fig. 16)

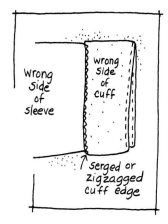

(labels in Fig. 16: wrong side of sleeve; wrong side of cuff; serged or zigzagged cuff edge)

Fig. 16

Turn the cuff to the right side of the jacket and topstitch around the sleeve on the pressed edge. Where the cuff meets at the sleeve placket, turn under and press the denim to miss the sleeve snaps or buttonholes and stitch in place.

3. For extra trim, sew belt loops and large buttons to the cuff edges as shown in the photograph.

SCATTERED STARS TENNIS SHOES

1. Use the small star applique pattern on page 32 to make individual small stars. I cut three of varying shades of denim for each shoe, but you may want fewer or more. Use permanent spray adhesive to attach the stars. Attach decorative nail heads by pushing the nail head prongs to the wrong side, then bend the prongs over using the rounded tip of a tea-spoon. Refer to the photo for place-ment ideas. Have fun wearing your jacket and matching shoes!

"I like to work with a theme when decorating clothing. I think of a theme or an event that I'd like an outfit for, and then I go for it. Maybe my next jacket will become a 'Gar-den Jacket' that features flowers and watch pocket flower pots or a crop blooming from the waistband rows. For a patriotic occasion, I could alter this jacket by rearranging the stars or substituting one of Mary's appliques. Whatever your preference in design themes, accept no limits and sew for the mood or the season. Adopt one of my sewing philosophies which is *'Never throw it away!'* because it will probably end up in a sewing project someday. Don't forget the men's clothing departments, find those bar-gains, and most of all, enjoy your creativity." - Luveta Nickels

Scattered Stars Tennis Shoes
To complete the outfit, trim a pair of tennis shoes to coordinate with the jacket. Add pizzazz with star appliques glued to the shoes and a new pair of red shoelaces.

Denim Chenille Collar

Stack layers of denim and chambray, sew them together, and slash them apart between the seamlines to create "chenille" fabric. The amazing part begins after cutting the layers open and tossing the new piece of fabric you created in the washer and dryer. The raveling and ruffling of the fabrics create the chenille appearance with great texture and dimension. The piece of denim chenille you create can be used for trimming denim and chambray garments.

Supplies to Gather:

Denim vest with plain neckline

Pieces of denim and chambray fabrics to layer and stitch

Ruler or grid marker

Chalk marker or washable marking pen

Scissors or Clover Slash Cutter

Mesh laundry bag

Steps to Take:

1. Practice this stitching before you start on an actual project. Cut layers of thick and thin denims, lightweight chambray, other colors of denim, whatever you have (I used three layers). Cut the bottom layer slightly larger than the top layers. This will help later when you're ready to cut through the fabrics. For layering denim chenille on other garments, I found thinner and fewer layers of denim - with chambray included for color contrast - to be the best weight with the least bulk. For the collar featured on the vest, I used chambray as the bottom or base fabric and added another layer of chambray with a top layer of lightweight blue denim.

2. Draw the first diagonal line on the bias of the top fabric using either a chalk marker or a washable

Denim Chenille Collar Vest with a Denim Chrysanthemum
A simple unlined vest becomes a specialty garment with the addition of a collar made from stitched and slashed layers of denim. As an extra touch of trim, pin or sew on a chrysanthemum made from extra scraps of denim fabric.

marking pen. Using a ruler or grid marker, draw the rest of the lines 1/2" apart. Stack the layers together and pin in a few places. (Fig. 1)

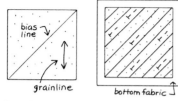

Fig. 1

3. Straight stitch on the diagonal lines, sewing with a 2.5 or 2.0 stitch length. You can experiment with different thread colors if you want contrasting color stitching on the top fabric. After all the lines are stitched, cut through all the layers of fabric except the bottom layer, cutting halfway between the rows of stitching. (Fig. 2) You will begin to see the edges lifting but this effect will become more apparent after washing and drying the piece of fabric.

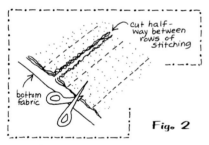

Fig. 2

4. Place the fabric in a mesh bag to wash and dry it. The bag will hold in lots of extra bits of fuzz that the fabric will shed in the laundering process.

5. To prepare the fabrics for this vest collar, make a pattern for the area to be covered with chenille. Use the collar pattern on page 39 as a guide and adjust according to your vest. Cut fabric pieces large enough to accommodate the collar pattern piece, with the bottom layer slightly larger. Add 1" all around to allow for shrinkage.

6. For the collar on the vest, I wanted the lines of stitching and fraying to come together at the vest

center front, so I planned the fabric pieces with "v" stitching lines. The first line marked on the top fabric was the center line. From this line, I marked bias lines 1/2" apart on each side, with the bias lines meeting at the center. (Fig. 3) This marking job is easy and quick to accomplish with the June Tailor Grid Marker (as seen in the photo below).

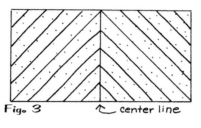

Fig. 3   ↰ center line

7. Pin the grid-marked top layer to the other layers of fabric. Sew the "v" stitching line marked on the fabric. Cut the stitched fabric in half along the straight center line first marked on the fabric. You now have two fabric pieces to slash open and cut the collars from after laundering.

8. With scissors or the Clover Slash Cutter, cut between the stitching lines through all but the bottom layer. Launder in a mesh bag. Cut the collar pattern from each piece of chenille fabric, making sure the lines

of slashing are in the correct direction for each side of the collar.

9. Sew the right side of the collar neck edge to the wrong side of the vest front, using a very narrow seam, less than 1/4". Press the seam and flip the collar to the front of the vest. Pin in position and zig-zag with clear thread to secure each collar piece. (Fig. 4)

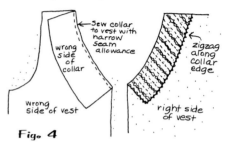

Fig. 4

When cut on the bias, denim has a naturally interesting frayed edge. Use this feature to advantage by making this layered fabric. Consider covering a pocket or a jacket collar with chenille, or making a new placket cover on a shirt. Once you try this technique, you're sure to dream up many other combinations. The collar is trimmed with another denim texture, a denim chrysanthemum.

Denim Chenille Samples and Experiments

Practice is always a good idea when trying new sewing techniques.

Here are some of the chenille combinations I created by layering, marking, and sewing different shades of denim together, cutting between the stitching lines, and washing the layered fabrics. To mark the bias lines on denim, the Grid Marker by June Tailor was a great tool. A pink or other light colored chalk marker made it easy to see the lines.

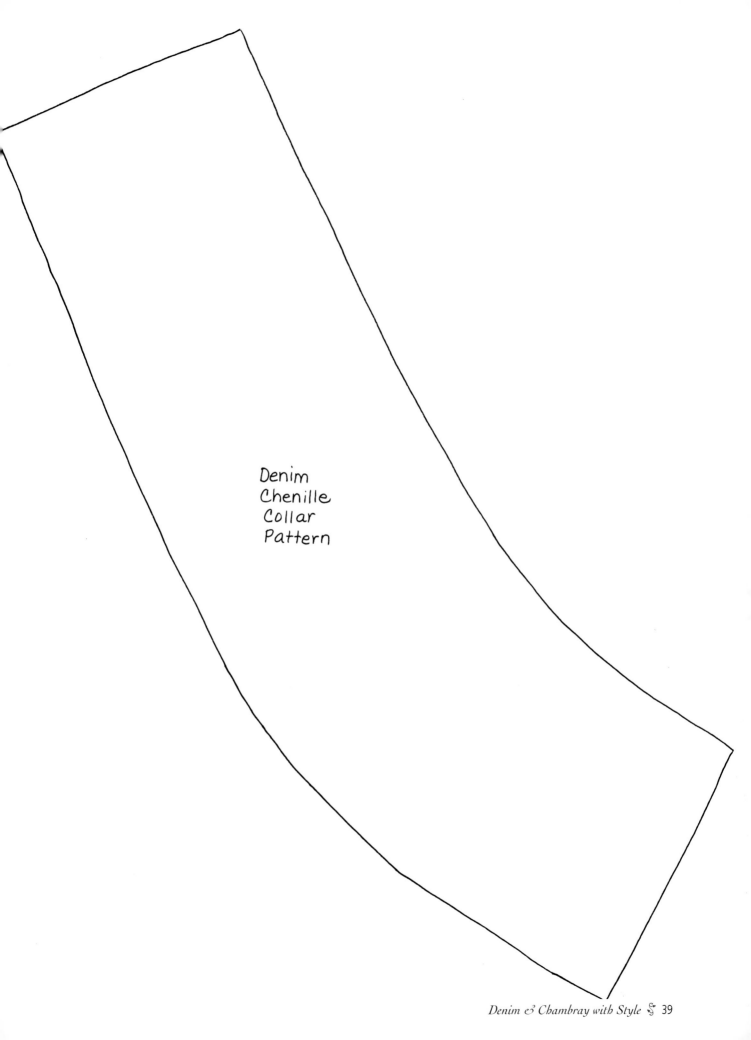

Denim
Chenille
Collar
Pattern

Denim Chrysanthemums

Use new or old denim circles to create a curled up flower with lots of texture. The flowers can be sewn or pinned to any hat, garment, or accessory.

Hats with Denim Chrysanthemums

See the possibilities for these fabric flowers on hats. Pin or sew the flowers to a hat band, ribbon, or directly to the hat. When you pin them on, they're easy to move to another location you want to trim. Ribbons by C.M. Offray.

Supplies to Gather:

Assorted denim weights and colors, including old jeans

Mesh laundry bag

Steps to Take:

1. Using the 3" circle pattern, cut five denim circles (or four, if using heavyweight denim) and stack them together on a base piece of denim. You can alternate the right and wrong sides of the denim when stacking them. Fold the top circle into quarters and press. Follow the foldlines to sew two intersecting lines 1" long through the center. (Fig. 1)

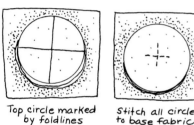

Top circle marked by foldlines

Stitch all circles to base fabric

Fig. 1

2. Cutting each layer individually, cut lines toward the center of the circles. There's no need to measure or try to do each layer the same since it's best if all the edges of the cuts don't line up. You can also cut the base fabric in the shape of one or more leaves. (Fig. 2)

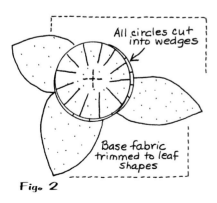

All circles cut into wedges

Base fabric trimmed to leaf shapes

Fig. 2

3. At this point, the circles aren't very impressive and the flower has no form. But assemble and sew several stacks of circles, throw them into a mesh laundry bag and let them go through a cycle in the washer and at least a partial cycle in the dryer.

4. The fun part comes when you open the mesh bag and discover the flowers. The bag holds in lots of threads and limits the mess in the laundering process.

5. Trim away excess base fabric if you don't want it to show. Sew or pin your fluffy edged flowers to a hat band, hair clip, vest (see page 37) or anything you'd like to trim with a dimensional flower.

Experiment with different colors and weights of denim for a flower shape that pleases you. In my experience, no fabric works as well as denim for this flower.

3" Circle pattern for denim Chrysanthemums

Denim Chrysanthemums in Stages

Start by sewing a stack of denim circles to a fabric base, then cut each circle into wedges, cutting toward the center. To get the curling edges of a flower, place the cut circles into a mesh laundry bag and launder it. When you open the bag, you'll be delighted with the textured, fluffy flower.

Frayed Denim Trim

Strips of denim cut on the bias turn into interesting textured trim after laundering. Sew the strips to the edges of a garment for a fast way to add unique detail.

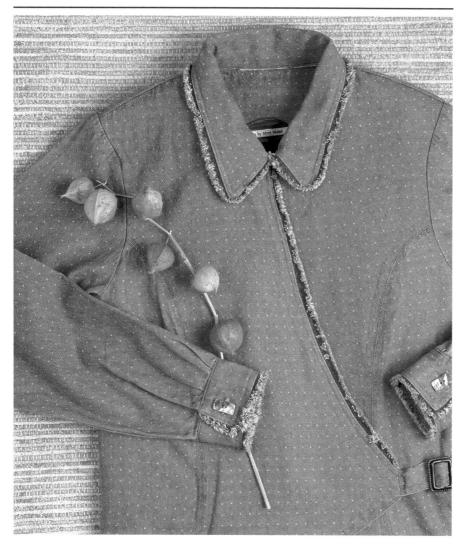

Frayed Denim Trim on a Shirt

Bias cut strips of denim, when treated to the laundry, develop an interesting controlled frayed edge. Sew the strips to the edges of a shirt, as you see here, for tone-on-tone trim.

Supplies to Gather:

Denim shirt

Denim pieces of different weights and colors

Mesh laundry bag

Denim needle

Steps to Take:

1. With a rotary cutter or scissors, cut 2" wide strips of denim on the bias. Cut the strips to the length needed for the edging on your garment, remembering that each strip will be cut in half. I recommend cutting several different colors and weights to wash all at the same time and test the fraying effect. You'll have a nice stash of frayed trim ready for decorating projects when the laundry is done.

2. Place all the strips in a mesh bag for laundering. The bag will hold in the extra threads and fuzz that are produced by washing and drying.

3. After the strips are dry, press them and cut them in half (1" wide) to make the trim for a garment. (Fig. 1)

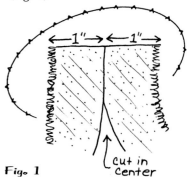

Fig. 1

4. Pin the right side of the strip to the wrong side of the garment edge with some of the denim showing as well as the frayed area. The frayed strips will ease well around curves since the strips are on the bias. With a denim needle on the machine, sew two seams to best secure the bias, the first seam 1/4" from the edge and the second seam right on the edge. (Fig. 2)

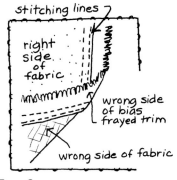

Fig. 2

Another idea for the washed strips: Instead of cutting them in half, sew a basting seam in the center to gather and make a ruffle.

Denim Fringe Trim

Cut and launder bias strips of denim to produce hanging fringe with a frayed edge. Instead of sewing the cut strips to the garment and then laundering everything, it's easiest to cut, wash, and dry the fringe strips and then attach them to the garment.

Denim Fringe as Yoke Trim
A bias cut piece of denim cut into fringe and laundered becomes a curly, frayed strip to trim a shirt yoke. A strip of narrow decorative braid adds an additional accent.

Supplies to Gather:

Denim shirt with back yoke seam

Mid to heavy weight denim in light to dark shades

Mesh laundry bag

Steps to Take:

1. Cut 3" wide bias strips of denim. If your fabric is not large enough to cut bias for the length you need on a garment, cut smaller 3" wide pieces and sew them together before cutting the fringe.

2. With right sides together, sew two strips with a straight line seam. Sew and reinforce the stitches at the top 1" of the strips and sew all the way down. (Fig. 1)

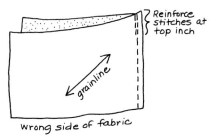

Fig. 1

Press the seam flat and mark 1" from the top edge of the fringe. Cut the seam off from the bottom, cutting right up against the stitching line, to the mark, then cut through the seam allowance as illustrated.

Add more stitching to the 1" section and press the seam allowance open on the wrong side. (Fig. 2)

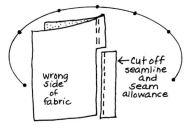

Fig. 2

3. Cut the fringe 1/2" wide and up to 1" from the top edge of the strip. If you cut the fringe narrower than 1/2", the fringe will tear apart easily. If you have pieced the strips together, start cutting the fringe from the opening of the piecing seam and cut in both directions. (Fig. 3)

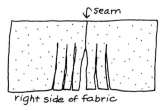

Fig. 3

4. Place the strips you've cut in a mesh laundry bag, wash in the automatic washer and dry in the dryer. Shake the mesh bag and the strips of fringe over a wastebasket to remove the extra bits of thread.

5. If the fringe ends are twisted and curled and you'd like to flatten them, press the strips while the denim is still damp. Pressing on the right side of the fabric, push the edge of the iron over the 1" top uncut edge toward the fringe and it will flatten and straighten out.

6. To sew the fringe to a garment, turn under the top edge and stitch on the folded edge. (Fig. 4)

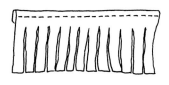

Fig. 4

I added a strip of narrow decorative braid below the top edge of the trim on the back of a shirt yoke. Future raveling of the denim will be minimal, but if you want to protect the fringe, wash the garment inside out when it needs laundering.

Fringe is fun and oh-so-easy with this method. When you're ready to try this technique, cut several strips and launder them together and save the extras for another project.

POCKET OPTIONS

pockets from

kimonos

basket

jacket

sunflower

bib jumper

arrangements

flower

Pockets from Kimonos

Cut from new and old Japanese fabrics, a pocket collection creates a stylish patch of trim on a denim top. Use the idea on other kinds of garments and accessories too. A plain tote bag front would look more interesting and serve more uses with a pocket collection to store small things. This denim top is further decorated with bias binding around the neck as well as an added back neck facing. The same Japanese print on the center pocket was used for the binding and facing.

Pockets from Kimonos

Collect vintage kimono fabrics or Japanese prints to build this combination of unique pockets to trim a denim shirt. A bias band of neck trim and a coordinating back neck facing add extra embellishment. The pocket fabrics are from Hoffman and Ah! Kimono (see Resources).

Supplies to Gather:

Denim pullover top

Small pieces of fabric for pockets and pocket tabs

Thread to match pocket fabrics, or clear nylon thread

2 buttons for pocket tabs

Optional: Small piece of Velcro for pocket closure

Steps to Take:

1. Trace the three pocket patterns on page 48. Refer to the patterns for cutting dimensions of the pocket tab and button loop. Add seam allowances and cut three pockets, one tab, and one button loop from various fabrics. Use the pocket arrangement in the photo as a guide or arrange the pockets to suit your own style. Note that the two dark pockets overlap the center pocket. Plan to pin and sew the overlapping edges to the center pocket before sewing any pockets to the garment. (Fig. 1)

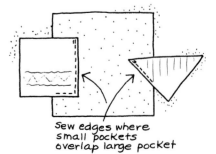

Sew edges where small pockets overlap large pocket

Fig. 1

2. Turn under and press the raw edges of the three pockets. Position and topstitch them to the garment.

3. Fold the pocket tab fabric in half lengthwise with right sides together. Sew across one short end and along the side as shown. (Fig. 2)

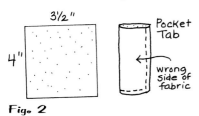

Fig. 2

Turn right side out for a tab 1-1/2" wide. Notice that the tab is not in the middle of the center pocket. Turn under and press the raw edge of the tab and sew the top of the tab to the garment. Sew a buttonhole in the tab, or sew Velcro to both the back of the tab and the pocket front. (Fig. 3) Sew a button to the pocket or the tab, as appropriate.

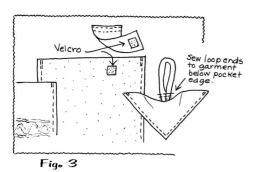

Fig. 3

4. Fold the button loop fabric in half lengthwise with right sides together and sew up the side. Turn right side out for a loop 1/2" wide and 4" long. (Fig. 4)

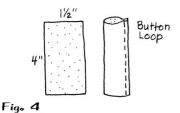

Fig. 4

Sew the raw fabric ends of the loop strip to the garment inside the triangle pocket (see Fig. 3). Sew the button to the pocket layer only.

5. To create the neckline facing, first turn the garment inside out to trace the back neck edge and shoulder lines on tracing or tissue paper. Refer to the Workshop section on page 121 for pattern making information. Cut a facing from fabric that dips to 5" at the bottom center. (Fig. 5) Turn under the edges of the facing and sew or serge the facing bottom edge. Attach the facing by placing it right side up inside the neckline and sewing close to the top neck edge.

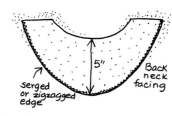

Fig. 5

6. Now it's time to add the bias. Cut a piece of bias fabric slightly longer than the neckline circumference and 1-3/4" wide. Press the fabric strip in half lengthwise with wrong sides together. Pin the cut edges of the bias at the top of the neckline edge on the right side of the garment, overlapping the ends that meet. (Fig. 6)

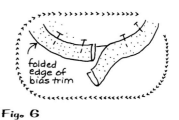

Fig. 6

Sew with a 1/4" seam allowance. Turn the folded edge of the bias fabric inside the neckline and pin in place. Trim away the excess fabric where the bias ends meet. Sew in the ditch between the garment and the bias from the right side of the garment to secure the bias. (Fig. 7)

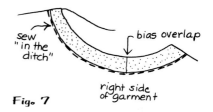

Fig. 7

A very ordinary denim garment takes on a sense of style with Japanese fabric trims. If you have a collection of special "precious-to-you" fabrics, consider highlighting them in a pocket collection and/or neckline trim. You'll enjoy seeing and wearing the fabrics instead of only occasionally petting them in your fabric stash. See the Resources section on page 126 for a kimono fabric source.

Pockets from Kimonos Patterns *

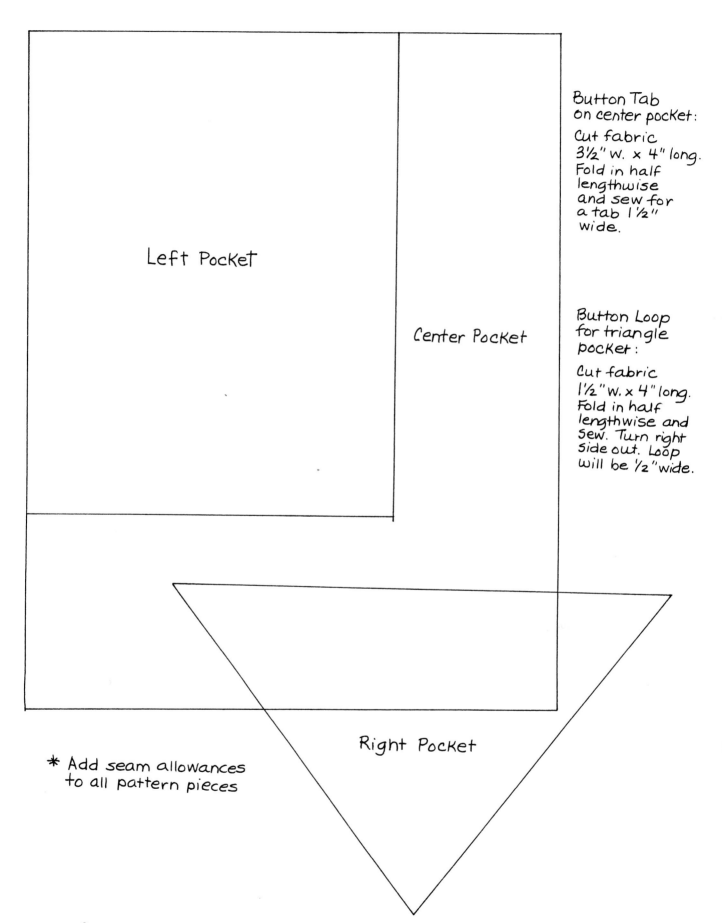

Left Pocket

Center Pocket

Button Tab on center pocket:
Cut fabric 3½" w. x 4" long. Fold in half lengthwise and sew for a tab 1½" wide.

Button Loop for triangle pocket:
Cut fabric 1½" w. x 4" long. Fold in half lengthwise and sew. Turn right side out. Loop will be ½" wide.

Right Pocket

* Add seam allowances to all pattern pieces

Basket Jacket

Turn a work jacket into a garment perfect for a gardener or basket lover. Each pocket becomes a basket with a fabric overlay, and collar and cuffs become more stylish with bright covers.

Supplies to Gather:

Denim work jacket with front pockets

Assorted fabrics for baskets, appliques, collar and cuff coverings

Threads to match fabrics, or clear nylon thread

Green fusible bias for flower stems

Denim needle

Scrap of green Ultrasuede or other nonfraying fabric for leaves and buttonhole covers

1/2 yd. stabilizer

Steps to Take:

1. Trace the pocket shapes from the jacket. Refer to the photo for the basket shapes I used. Patterns for these shapes are on page 52 and may be adapted for your jacket. Make each basket shape larger than the actual pockets to allow clearance of any riveted corners or heavily stitched areas.

2. Cut baskets from fabric, adding a 1/2" seam allowance on all edges. Also cut 1" wide strips of bias fabric for the basket handles. The basket at the jacket left bottom edge has a 12" handle and the upper basket has a 9-1/2" handle. Turn under the long edges of the bias strips and press. Also press the strip into a

Basket Jacket

Cover the ordinary pockets on a work jacket with colorful printed fabrics to create baskets. Additional trim includes basket handles, flowers, and bows. To continue improving the jacket, cover the collar and cuffs and frame the buttonholes with triangles of fabric. This colorful jacket is a day brightener. All the cotton fabrics are by Hoffman.

semicircle to curve from one edge of the pocket to the other. Place a piece of stabilizer inside the jacket under the area where the basket handle will be sewn. Pin the curved bias strip to the jacket and blanket stitch it on both the inner and outer edges, using clear nylon thread.

3. Turn under and press the seam allowances on the basket shapes. Note that the upper basket is made from a block of Wedge Seminole Patchwork, as explained on page 27. The upper edge of the basket fabric will line up with the pocket edge. Pin and sew the fold of the seam allowance to the pocket edge so that the basket fabric's right side is covering the handle area. (Fig. 1)

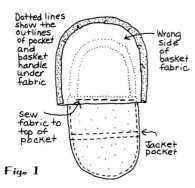

Fig. 1

This will be an awkward seam to sew, and you'll need to avoid sewing on rivets or secured corners, but it's the best way to secure the fabric edge to the pocket with a hidden seam. Flip the fabric back over the pocket and pin and sew the other edges in place on the jacket.

4. Trace the applique bow pattern on page 51. If you cut the bow from Ultrasuede you won't have to turn under the edges before topstitching it to the jacket. For applique instructions, see page 120 of the Workshop section.

5. Make a handle for the flower basket by cutting a 5" x 3" piece of fabric, folding it in half, and sewing it as illustrated. (Fig. 2) Turn it right side out and sew one short edge to

the jacket and the other edge to the basket edge. Add a button for trim.

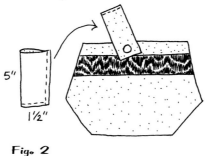
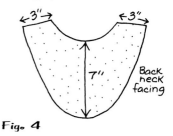

Fig. 2

6. For the flower stems, cut and fuse pieces of fusible green bias tape onto the jacket. Stitch with clear nylon thread or green thread to match the bias tape. For the flowers, use pinking shears to cut 1-1/2" diameter circles from fabric. Sew the circles to the ends of the stems by stitching the circles in quarters. (Fig. 3)

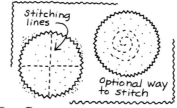

Fig. 3

This simple attachment will allow the edges to stand out. There may be some fraying after wearing and laundering, but that will add dimension to the flowers. Use the leaf pattern on page 52 and cut leaves from Ultrasuede. Stitch the leaves on with straight stitching in a vein pattern instead of sewing around the edges as you usually would.

7. The top pocket has an old hanky inserted. Pencils, small gardening tools, or sunglasses could also be stored in the basket pocket.

8. Make a new back neck facing for the jacket. Use the pattern tracing instructions in the Workshop section on page 121 to trace the neck curve and shoulder seams of the jacket on tissue or tracing paper. Add a 1/4" seam allowance at the neck edge. Cut the facing 7" wide at the center and

taper up to 3" at the shoulder seams. (Fig. 4) Pin and sew the facing, right side up, to the inside of the jacket with the neckline seam allowance extending up onto the collar.

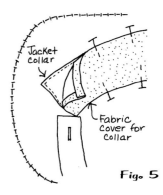

Fig. 4

9. Trace the collar of the jacket on tissue or tracing paper, using the techniques in the Workshop section on page 121. Add 1/2" seam allowances on all sides of the collar before cutting it from fabric. Pin the middle of the collar fabric, right side up, to the right side of the jacket collar. Turn under and pin the fabric edges to meet the collar at the outside edges. (Fig. 5)

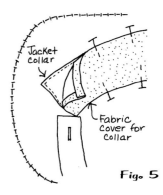

Fig. 5

Sew in place. As an afterthought, I added a wavy band of fabric to the top of the collar. I used a wide blanket stitch and contrasting color thread to attach the trim. If you plan the collar better than I did, you could sew the trim to the collar fabric before you attach it to the jacket.

10. For the cuff linings, turn the sleeves wrong side out to trace the sleeve end. I cut a fabric band 7" wide and the length around the sleeve plus 1/2" for seam allowances. Sew the cuff fabric into a tube and turn under and press the open

edges. Pin the wrong side of the fabric to the wrong side of the sleeve and sew at both the cuff edges to attach the cuff to the jacket. (Fig. 6)

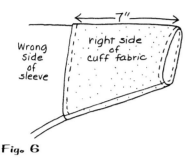

Fig. 6

I used two different fabrics for the cuff linings. Why not? The fashion police will not detain you if your cuffs are not lined with the same fabric. Roll the fabric cuffs back over the jacket's sleeve ends.

11. Buttonhole covers. Trace the triangle pattern below and cut as many triangles as there are buttonholes on the jacket. I cut the covers from Ultrasuede for a strong and colorful addition to the jacket front. Spray fuse or use paper-backed fusible web to attach the covers over the buttonholes. Sew the triangles from the wrong side of the buttonholes, using a narrow zigzag stitch. Cut the buttonholes open from the wrong side of the jacket. (Fig. 7)

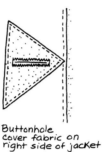

Fig. 7

Buttonhole
cover fabric on
right side of jacket

12. I left the riveted buttons on the jacket. I could have cut them off, added fabric to cover the holes, and sewn on different buttons. See the instructions for this on page 122.

If you have time to make another basket, add it to the back of the jacket. No one will ever call this a boring old denim jacket!

Buttonhole
Cover

Bow for Basket
Handle

Basket Jacket Patterns

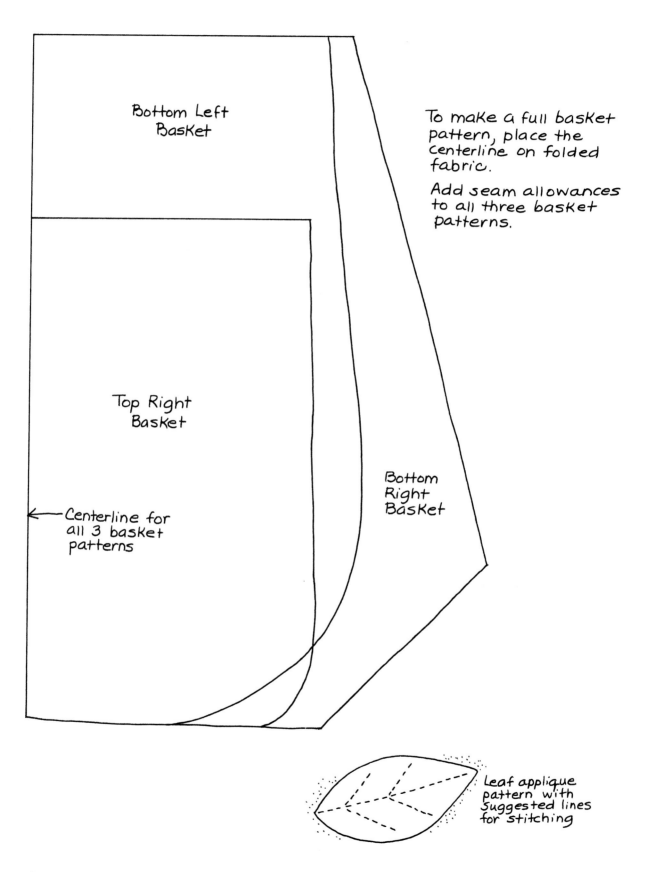

Bottom Left
Basket

Top Right
Basket

← Centerline for
all 3 basket
patterns

Bottom
Right
Basket

To make a full basket
pattern, place the
centerline on folded
fabric.

Add seam allowances
to all three basket
patterns.

Leaf applique
pattern with
suggested lines
for stitching

Sunflower Bib Jumper

Just ignore the bib front pocket and sew an applique over the top! Of course you have to pay attention to metal rivets or buttons, but they can be cut off and the area covered with a thick fabric applique, such as the felt ones used for this design. I placed the sunflower to the side to keep the pencil pocket functional on the jumper. New buttons on the side opening coordinate with the colors of the applique.

Supplies to Gather:

Denim bib jumper

Felt, corduroy, Polarfleece, or other thick fabrics for applique

Thread to match fabrics, or clear nylon thread

Denim needle

Fusible spray

Four buttons to match applique fabric

Steps to Take:

1. Remove any riveted buttons or metal trim from the bib pocket area by cutting with small sharp scissors very close to the rivet or button. See the Workshop section on page 122. Plan to cover the area with part of the applique.

2. Trace the sunflower pattern on page 54 onto paper. Cut the different sections (petals, leaves and stem, flower center) from appropriate fabrics. I recommend using thick fabrics so the lines and edges of the bib pockets won't show through the applique.

3. Spray the back of the applique shapes with fusible spray and assemble the design parts on the pocket area. Stabilizer is usually not necessary for stitching on the bib. Use the flower position in the photo as a placement guide.

Sunflower Bib Jumper

If you don't need to use the pockets, sew over them! I chose textured felt by Kunin for the sunflower. The pencil pocket remains open to use for its intended purpose.

4. Sew around the edges of all parts of the design, using clear or matching thread and a narrow zigzag or blanket stitch. You will sew through all layers of fabric - applique, pocket, and garment - so be sure to use the denim needle on the sewing machine and sew slowly. These stitches will be hidden in the thick fabric edges.

5. Cut off the riveted metal buttons in the side opening of the jumper, following the instructions in step 1. (Fig. 1a) Wrap the placket where the buttons were with fabric on the front and back and sew on the new cover. (Fig. 1b) Now sew on the replacement buttons. This bibbed garment is sure to look a lot better!

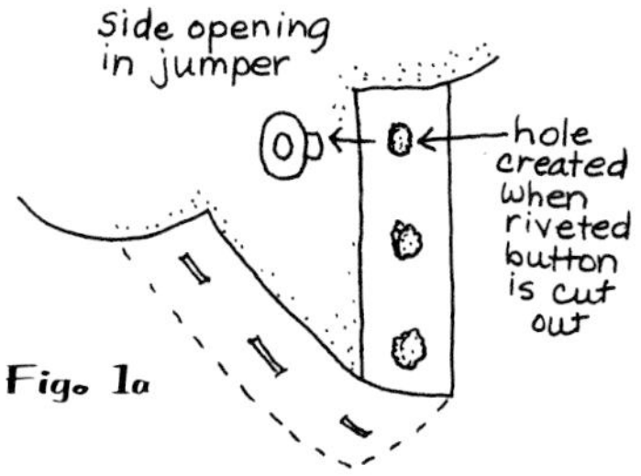

Side opening in jumper

hole created when riveted button is cut out

Fig. 1a

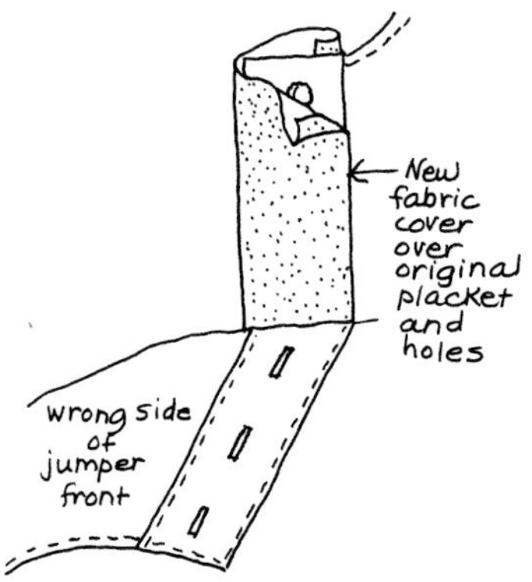

New fabric cover over original placket and holes

wrong side of jumper front

Fig. 1b

It would take a lot of hard work and dedicated ripping to remove the pocket from a bibbed garment to sew on an applique, so skip all that work and just stitch a design over the top of the pocket. You can plan the design layout to keep a working pocket, such as the pencil pocket on the bibbed jumper pictured.

Sunflower Applique Pattern

Flower Arrangements on a Denim Dress

A classic-style denim dress features two chest pockets. While it's tempting to repeat the same design on both sides of the dress, an unbalanced design is much more interesting. Purchased fabric yo-yos become simple flowers with stems created with repositionable bias tape. There are more flowers on the bottom of the skirt, arranged in a denim basket cut from an old pair of jeans.

Supplies to Gather:

Denim dress with front pockets

Fabric yo-yos, purchased or handmade

Green double-fold bias tape

1/4 yd. double stick paper-backed fusible web (Steam A Seam 2 or AppliqEase)

Clear nylon thread or thread to match stems and bow

Small piece of fabric for bow

6.0 double needle

Chalk marker

Pocket and belt loops cut from old jeans

Fusible spray

Denim needle

Flower Arrangements on a Dress

Fabric yo-yos become simple flowers in two areas on this classic denim dress. Stems are easy to make with fusible bias tape you buy or make yourself. Use a pocket as a flower holder or the pocket cut from a pair of jeans. The dress is by Sunbelt.

Flowers in a Pocket

An appliqued bow appears to hold five flower stems that spread across the dress front. Try the dress on to plan the flower display for a flattering arrangement. The yo-yo flowers are from Wimpole Street Creations (see Resources).

Flower Basket from Old Jeans

A jeans pocket and five belt loops form a flower basket on the skirt of the denim dress. Place the bias flower stems over or under the belt loop basket handle and pin or sew yo-yos at the ends of the stems.

Steps to Take:

1. Using the dress in the photo as a guide, draw lines with a chalk marker for the flower stems on the dress top. (Fig. 1) Try on the dress to make sure the flowers placed at the ends of the stems will not fall directly on the bustline.

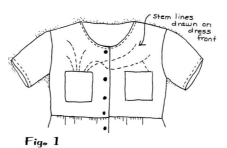

Fig. 1

2. Several projects in this book make use of pre-made fusible bias tape. Green bias tape is available in this form, but for this dress I wanted to use a different shade of green for the stems. With double stick paper-backed fusible webs it's possible to make your own repositionable and fusible bias tape from any color of bias. I used double-fold green bias and cut away about half of one side of the tape to eliminate an extra layer of fabric. (Fig. 2) Make sure to press the bias tape flat, especially if it has been stored and wrapped around a card.

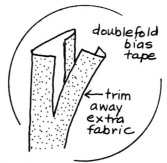

Fig. 2

3. Cut narrow strips of double stick paper-backed fusible web, remove one layer of paper and finger press it to the wrong side of the bias tape.

Peel away the second layer of paper. Now the bias has a tacky back and can be finger pressed on the lines on the dress and moved if you don't like the original placement. On the left side of the dress, place the stem ends into the pocket at least 3/4". For the stems that cross over the dress front, cut longer pieces to wrap around the dress front edge. On the other side of the dress front, place the end of the bias stem behind the front placket area and carefully line it up with the stem on the other side of the dress.

4. When the placement is correct, fuse the stems in place. Now you're ready to sew.

5. With the 6.0 double needle on the machine and two spools of clear nylon or green thread to match the bias, adjust the machine to a narrow zigzag stitch. Press the double needle safety button if your machine has that feature. This prevents the double needles from swinging over too far and breaking as they hit the presser foot or machine bed. Ouch!

6. You may want to practice this stitch before working on the dress. Place a piece of the fusible bias on a scrap of fabric and sew on the edges to secure the bias in one sewing step. When you feel confident, sew the bias strips to the dress. (Fig. 3)

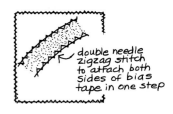

Fig. 3

7. Sew fabric yo-yos to the ends of the stems. Refer to the illustration for instructions to make your own. (Fig. 4)

Make Your Own Yo-yos

Cut this pattern from fabric. Turn under and press the edge 1/4" to the wrong side of fabric.

Hand sew around the seam allowance with a running stitch. Pull the threads to gather. Knot the threads.

Fig. 4

11. Draw flower stem lines for your basket flower arrangement. Refer to the photo as a guide. Notice that some stems are stitched over the belt loop handle and other stems go under the loops. (Fig. 7) Refer to steps 3-5 to apply and sew the bias tape. Sew yo-yos to the tops of the stems.

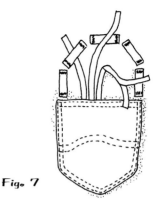

Fig. 7

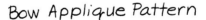

Here are other ways to create embellishments. Instead of yo-yos, sew or pin on buttons. Tie a wire-edged ribbon around one of the belt loops of the basket. Sew several jeans pocket baskets to the skirt bottom for a circle of baskets. Pockets from different sizes of jeans would be an interesting feature too.

8. Trace the bow applique pattern on this page and cut it from fabric. Spray the back with fusible spray, attach it to the upper edge of the pocket and sew. You can sew the bow only to the pocket, or, if you don't plan to use the pocket, stitch through both the pocket and the dress fabric. For applique instructions, see page 120 in the Workshop section.

9. For the skirt basket, cut a denim pocket from an old pair of jeans. Cut the pocket off the denim fabric rather than ripping out the pocket stitching. Trim away the fabric around the pocket and from inside the pocket. (Fig. 5)

wrong side of belt loop

Fig. 6

10. On the skirt, arrange the pocket and belt loops as a basket with a handle. With clear thread and a denim needle on the machine, zigzag the pocket edges and belt loop ends to the dress.

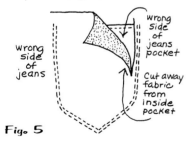

wrong side of jeans

wrong side of jeans pocket

Cut away fabric from inside pocket

Fig. 5

Cut the belt loops off the jeans by cutting them off the waistband rather than undoing the stitches. Trim away as much extra jeans fabric as you can from the back of the belt loops. (Fig. 6)

Bow Applique Pattern

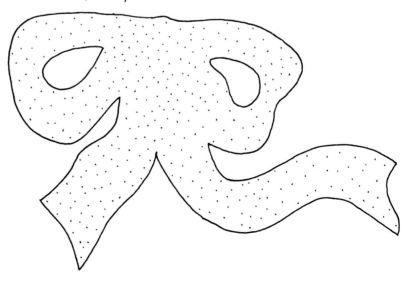

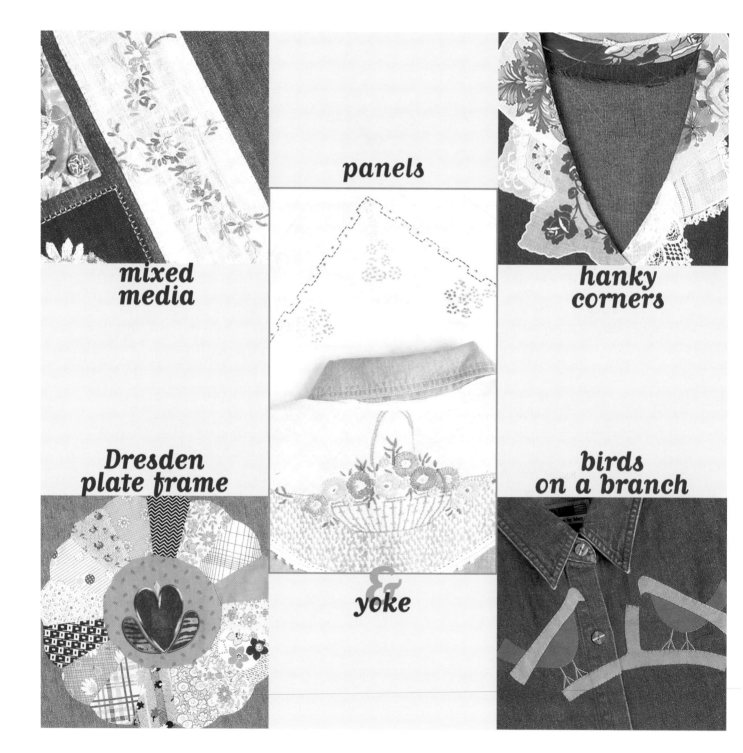

mixed media

panels

hanky corners

Dresden plate frame

yoke

birds on a branch

&

Vintage Linen Panels & Yoke

Whether they're from your personal collection of old linens or from a yard sale or antique store, vintage linens like dresser scarves, dinner napkins, tablecloths, and armchair covers make great additions to new clothing. Pieces with stains or holes or other problems usually have usable areas to cut out and use. The small tablecloth featured on the left side of the dress was priced at only $4 at an antique store because there were dark stains in several areas. I was delighted to salvage the piece and show just a corner of it as part of the dress trim.

Supplies to Gather:

Chambray dress

Three pieces of vintage linens for the dress front and back

Clear nylon or thread to match the linens

Steps to Take:

1. Use the picture as a guide for making patterns for the front panels and back yoke of the dress. The vintage linens you have for this project may dictate the size and placement of the panels. Use the instructions in the Workshop section on page 121 to make tissue patterns for both front panels and for the back yoke.

2. If there are pockets with buttons on the garment front, remove at least the buttons and possibly the pockets too to avoid extra bulk or lines beneath the panels. The tablecloth panel on the left covers the buttonhole area, and on the right, the panel is shorter and just covers the pocket edge. In other words, the two front panels do not have to match up exactly. (Fig. 1)

Dress with Vintage Linen Panels
Framed by a portion of the tablecloth used for one of its linen panels, this chambray dress takes on a new life with its old trims. An embroidered dresser scarf was used for the second and smaller panel on the dress front.

3. Position the pattern pieces on the vintage linens and cut out the panels with a wide seam allowance of 1" all around on the cut edges. (Fig. 2) I always find it's safest to cut a wider seam allowance in case I want to

Fig. 1

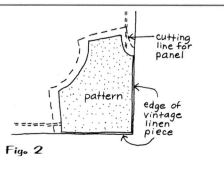

Fig. 2

move the piece to a slightly different position on the garment. You can always cut away any excess seam allowance before you sew. It goes along with the carpentry rule about measuring twice and cutting once! –

4. Pin the linen panel to the garment with many pins in the center and turn under the edges at the neckline, shoulder, armhole, and side seam. For curved edges, clip the seam allowance. (Fig. 3)

Fig. 3

If you use a crocheted-edge tablecloth for the back yoke as I did, you may want to retain the shape of the corner of the scarf with its decorated edge. At the shoulder line, the front and back linen panels will overlap so the first panels sewn in place can have the shoulder edges extended and not turned under. Pin and sew the back yoke first, then pin and sew the front panels to the garment. To test the hang and placement of the front panels, try on the garment before sewing them in place. You may decide to sew all edges of the panels to the garment so there are no loose

edges to move as you wear the garment. Just remember to keep the buttonhole area accessible for wearing the dress!

Another idea for vintage linen panels on the garment front is to make them removable by buttoning them on around the neckline and at the shoulder. This way, you could make more than one set to interchange. Wouldn't the women who created these fabric works of art be happy to have us using their old work in very new ways?

Vintage Linen Dress Yoke

A scalloped and embroidered tablecloth corner was cut for the back yoke of the chambray dress. What a great way to feature the usable portions of vintage linens with frayed edges or stains!

Jumper with Hanky Corners

With a small collection of handkerchiefs, you can create an unusual edge trim for a jumper or any garment. Find hankies in your stash or at antique stores, estate and yard sales. This project is a great way to use and highlight the decorative corners of hankies, especially the ones with stains or holes in the centers.

Jumper with Hanky Corners

A collection of old handkerchiefs inspired the embellishment idea for this jumper from Sunbelt. Corners cut from the hankies form a pointed border around the neckline and front edge. I changed the buttons to blend with the fabric and make the hanky corners the focal point of the garment.

Steps to Take:

1. Start with the neckline edge of the jumper or other garment of your choice. Line up hanky corners around the neckline before cutting them. Plan to overlap edges and place some corners between two others, as shown on the jumper pictured. After settling on an arrangement of hanky corners, cut them from the hankies, leaving 1" beyond the neckline edge. The edge of this extension is on the bias, which makes it easier to fold over a curving neckline edge. (Fig. 1)

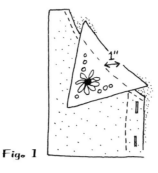

Fig. 1

2. Pin the 1" extensions to the inside of the neckline (wrong side of hanky to wrong side of garment), with the hanky points extending into the neckline. Sew two seams, 1/4" apart, to secure the hanky points to the jumper. (Fig. 2)

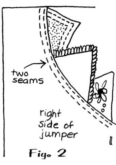

two seams

right side of jumper

Fig. 2

3. If you wish to clean up the back neckline edge of the garment so it has "hanger appeal" and no raw hanky edges, cut a piece of bias from the center of one of the hankies you have already cut. Turn under the long edges, press, and sew the bias strip in place by machine.

4. Fold the hanky points over the neckline edges and pin in place. Sew with a narrow zigzag around all points to hold them in place on the garment. (Fig. 3)

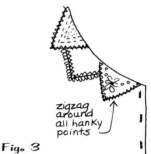

zigzag around all hanky points

Fig. 3

5. Cut hanky points with 1" extensions for the front opening of the jumper. Place the hanky points between the buttonholes. Alternate colors and styles of hankies. As you did at the neckline, pin the 1" extensions to the inside of the jumper and sew two seams to hold the edges to the garment. Fold the hanky corners over the garment edge, pin in place and sew with a narrow zigzag to secure.

Don't feel limited to using this technique on a jumper only. Any collarless neckline can be treated with hanky corners. Think about a vest, a dress, a round neck top, or even the edge of a wrap skirt. This is a great new way to enjoy your hanky collection.

Neckline Detail of Jumper with Hanky Corners
Hanky corners are positioned between the buttonholes and to encircle the neckline. A strip of bias cut from one of the hankies covers the raw edges of the hanky corners in the back neckline of the jumper.

Mixed Media Dress

Combine decorated "elements" to trim the front of a dress or other denim garment. On the dress pictured, I selected a floral theme. A rose from printed fabric, a section from an old dresser scarf, and a machine embroidery design are the mixed media depicting flowers.

Mixed Media Dress

Three different floral designs form the dress front display. The large rose on the left is a button-on design - look closely to see the buttons in the corners. Below the rose is a machine embroidery design by Singer. The third portion of the display is a section of an embroidered dresser scarf. The rose fabric is by Hoffman.

Steps to Take:

1. First make the removable button-on decoration shown on the upper left. To select a portion of a print fabric for a button-on design, use a window cut out of paper or a clear template to position on the fabric. The rose design on the dress is a 4" square of fabric. Trace the outline of the window or template and cut the fabric 1/4" larger all around to accommodate seam allowances. Cut a second piece of fabric the same size. You may wish to make this print square reversible. (Fig. 1)

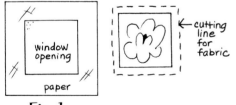

Window opening

paper

← cutting line for fabric

Fig. 1

2. Place the fabrics with right sides together. For square corners on the finished piece, stitch to the end of each side, turn under the seam allowance to the seamline and proceed to sew the next side. Leave a 1" opening on one side to turn right side out when the stitching is complete. Push out the corners and press the fabrics flat. If it's important to

you, seal the 1" opening with hand stitching or use a small piece of fusible web to fuse the opening. I have been known to press the opening and pretend I sewed it shut! (Fig. 2)

Seam #1 — Wrong side of fabric

Seam #2 — Wrong side of fabric

Wrong side of fabric — Seam #3

Wrong side of fabric — Seam #4

Fig. 2

Sew buttonholes in each corner of the square.

3. The machine embroidery in the lower left corner is done on a 5" square. The design shown in the photo was created with the embroidery unit on a sewing machine. Use embroideries you've stitched to fabric pieces for this part of the project. You can trim the embroidered fabric to 5" if you plan to satin stitch over the edge or turn under the fabric edges to prepare it for stitching to the garment.

4. The third piece is a section from an old and stained dresser scarf with floral embroidery. The section shown in the picture was clean and usable. I cut a section 4" wide and turned the long edges under before stitching. I left the lace edging on the top and bottom edges of the piece. On a light colored piece of linen, fuse lightweight fusible interfacing behind the design area so there's less see-through effect, especially when sewing the fabric to dark denim.

5. After preparing all the parts of the design, you're ready to sew them to

the garment. Pin the three pieces in place. It's always best to try on the dress or garment to mark the bust-line and test the trim arrangement before you sew. Pin the square with buttonholes to the dress and use chalk to mark the placement of the buttons through the buttonholes. Sew the buttons to the dress. How about using four different buttons?

6. Use paper-backed fusible web or fusible spray on the back of the machine embroidery design piece to secure it to the garment before sewing. Sew the square with rayon thread to match the thread in the embroidery. Sew with a decorative stitch such as the buttonhole stitch I chose. (Fig. 3) If the edges of the embroidered fabric are raw, satin stitch to cover the edges.

Buttonhole stitch sewn over turned under edge of embroidery design fabric.

Fig. 3

7. Treat the back of the dresser scarf section with either paper-backed fusible web or fusible spray so you can secure it to the garment. With clear nylon thread and a narrow zigzag or buttonhole stitch, sew around the edges to permanently attach it to the garment.

Build another mixed media design near the dress hemline or on the back of the garment. Even small pieces of embroidery from the past can be salvaged and turned into a classy decoration, and all pieces could be buttoned on.

Dresden Plate Frame for Embroidery

I found several Dresden plate quilt circles in a bag at an antique store. The edges were all turned under and ready to stitch, so I used one of the circles as shown in the picture to frame a piece of machine embroidery. You may have some of these circles in your old quilt scraps stash, or you can make a circle of your own to use as a frame. With vintage fabric prints now available at fabric and quilt stores, you can duplicate the look of an old quilt piece.

Supplies to Gather:

Denim garment with plain front or back

Dresden plate circle or pieces of 16 fabrics to make your own

A piece of machine embroidery or a design to frame in the center

Clear nylon thread

Fusible spray

Steps to Take:

1. To build your own Dresden plate circle, cut 16 pieces of fabric using the section pattern on page 66. A 1/4" seam allowance is included on all sides of the pattern. Arrange the 16 pieces in a circle and sew the side seams together. Turn under and press the inside and outside edges. To make it easier to turn the edges under, you may want to clip the seam allowances. (Fig. 1)

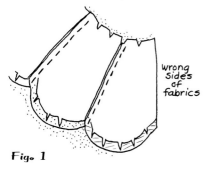

wrong sides of fabrics

Fig. 1

Dresden Plate Embroidery Frame
Centered in a circle of Dresden plate quilt pieces is a machine embroidery I designed for the Viking Sewing Machine Co. Use this idea to frame other embroideries, a monogram, or another small stitching project.

2. Center and pin the machine embroidery or other design in the center of the circle you made or found in your stash.

3. Spray the back of the circle and the embroidery with fusible spray.

Place and pin the pieces on a garment. This design idea works well on the front or back of a garment. With clear nylon thread and a small zigzag, first sew the inside circle to the garment, then sew around the outer circle curved edge.

Dresden
Plate
Pattern

1/4" seam
allowances

Cut 16 for a
full circle.

This quick and easy decorating idea can be enhanced with a thin layer of quilt batting beneath the center design area. You could also quilt the batting area by machine or hand to add another dimensional detail.

CUP OF
KINDNESS

More Ideas for Machine Embroideries and Denim

Sew and save embroidered designs for projects like these. The denim apron features four floral designs by Pfaff, with strips of decorative trim between them. The Mary Englebreit design was stitched on a Bernina machine and made into a pocket. The back of a denim shirt features three Brother embroideries in a floral theme.

Birds on a Branch Shirt

A kitchen towel I found at an antique store in Two Harbors, Minnesota, inspired the design featured on this sleeveless denim shirt. It's fun to use something old and make your own version with new fabrics.

Supplies to Gather:

Denim shirt with button front

Applique fabrics for bird/branch design (small pieces are adequate)

Paper-backed fusible web or fusible spray

1/4 yd. stabilizer

Optional: replacement buttons for shirt

Steps to Take:

1. Use the bird and branch design pattern on page 68 or challenge yourself to find and use a design from a piece of vintage linen you have in your own stash. You can duplicate the colors of the original design or plan the design to coordinate with the new buttons, as I did. I chose Ultrasuede as an updated fabric for my design, and sewed it on in two sections on a button-up shirt front. This is not the usual placement for a horizontal design, but part of the challenge of embellishing is finding new methods and design placements.

2. Trace the pattern provided or from your piece of vintage linen. Reduce or enlarge the design on a copy machine so it fits your garment. Plan the area where the design will split if you sew it to a button-front garment. (Fig. 1)

Birds on a Branch Shirt

An old dishtowel inspired the applique design on this shirt from Sunbelt. Check your stash of vintage linens for other ideas to use for applique.

Split the design and add an extension to each side of the branch for placement on split shirt front.

Fig. 1

Birds on a Branch Applique Pattern

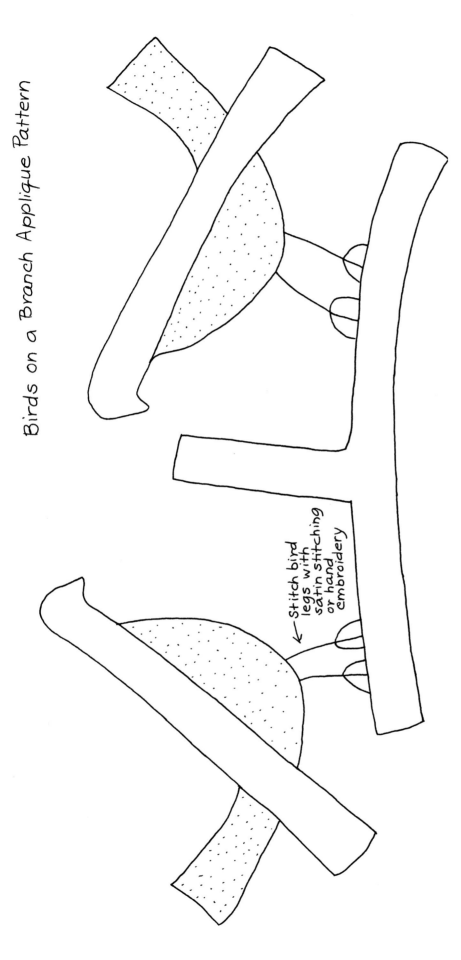

Stitch bird legs with satin stitching or hand embroidery

Trace the design in reverse on paper-backed fusible web and fuse the traced shapes to the wrong side of the applique fabrics. Cut out and peel off the paper backing. If you decide to use fusible spray instead, cut the design pieces from fabric and spray the wrong sides of the fabric with spray before positioning them on the garment.

3. Refer to the machine applique section in the Workshop of page 120 for specific applique instructions. Make sure there is a piece of stabilizer under the design area on the garment. Do the stitching and tear away the stabilizer.

This design can also be placed on the solid front or back of a dress, jumper, or other top, but it is interesting to break it into two pieces and use it on a button-up shirt front.

part 5

MOVABLE EMBELLISHMENTS

pieced details

slip-over stole

button-down

collar &

tuxedo bib

seasonal

Chambray Shirt with Pieced Details

An ordinary chambray shirt becomes extraordinary with extra layers of fabric to highlight the collar, cuffs, and placket. I chose cotton flannel for the trim, but any soft fabric would work. The final detail is simply buttoned on: button frames made from Ultrasuede. My sister Sarah is wearing this shirt in our family portrait on page 4.

Chambray Shirt with Pieced Details

Pieces of flannel fabrics cover the collar, cuffs, and placket of an ordinary chambray shirt. The button frames are a removable feature. In the family photo, my sister Sarah is wearing this shirt. She's an enthusiastic quilter and wild berry picker, so I added the fat quarters to the shirt pocket and a dish of Minnesota wild blueberries.

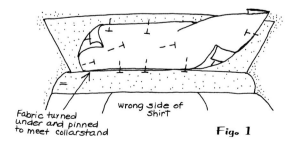

Fabric turned
under and pinned
to meet collarstand

wrong side of
shirt

Fig. 1

Supplies to Gather:

Chambray shirt

1/2 yd. fabric for trimming collar and cuffs, smaller piece for contrasting placket trim

Thread to match fabrics or clear nylon thread

1/4 yd. paper-backed fusible web

Ultrasuede scraps for button frames

Steps to Take:

1. Trace the collar on the shirt, using tissue or tracing paper. Refer to the tracing instructions in the Workshop section on page 121. Cut the collar shape from fabric without adding an extra seam allowance. By cutting the trim fabric the same size as the collar, you will have adequate fabric to turn under and still show the original collar edges.

2. Pin the collar fabric right side up across the center of the collar only. Turn under and pin the collar edge to meet the collarstand. (Fig. 1) If the seam allowance adds too much bulk, trim some away. On the other three edges of the collar, turn under the edges so that some of the original collar shows. I kept 1/2" of the original collar exposed and trimmed away some of the excess fabric from the turned-under seam allowance. After all the edges of the fabric are pinned in place, sew with a straight topstitch around the edges and remove the pins.

3. Use the same procedure on the cuffs. Trace one cuff and cut two pieces of fabric from your pattern. Pin the cuff fabric across the centers of the cuff and turn under the fabric edges. (Fig. 2) Notice in the photo that the extra cuff fabric aligns with the sleeve end of the cuff, and the original cuff fabric is left exposed on the other sides.

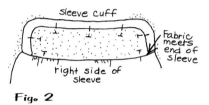

Fig. 2

4. By sewing fabric over the cuff, you will be covering the buttonholes. After the extra fabric is stitched on, sew around the buttonholes on the wrong side of the cuffs, using either a straight stitch or a very narrow zig-zag stitch. Cut the buttonholes open again from the wrong sides of the cuffs and sew the buttons back on the cuffs. (Fig. 3)

5. Now add strips of fabric down the center placket. Fuse paper-backed fusible web to a 20" long strip of 1/2" wide fabric. Of course you can change these measurements to fit the garment you are working on. Cut the long strip into pieces to fit between the buttonholes. Remove the paper backing and fuse each section into place on the shirt. (Fig. 4) Sew around each one with a satin stitch or another decorative stitch. If you have extra strips left, try placing them above or on the upper edge of the shirt pocket.

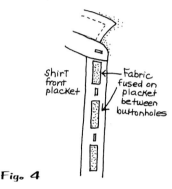

Fig. 4

6. The button frames are easy and clever. They'll make even normal, boring shirt buttons look more interesting. Use the pattern in Fig. 5 as a starting place for your frames. Note the position of the buttonhole so the Ultrasuede square becomes a diamond when the frames are buttoned on the shirt.

7. Depending on the buttons on the blouse, you may find that one or two layers of Ultrasuede work better. Experiment first with one layer of Ultrasuede. Carefully cut the buttonhole in the center, making sure you cut the buttonhole the exact size of the button and no larger. If buttonholes on the frames are too big, the frames slip off the buttons easily. I report this fact based on experience. If a single layer of Ultrasuede does not seem stable enough, fuse two layers of the fabric together, using paper-backed fusible web, then cut the buttonhole. Another possibility: change the buttons to accommodate a thicker Ultrasuede frame.

8. When you're not wearing the button frames, store them in the shirt pocket.

Keep these shirt details in mind for a shirt you like with problems on the collar, cuff, or placket. The extra fabric layers in these areas can successfully cover stains, tears, or worn areas and you'll extend the life of a shirt. The button frame idea can be created in a variety of shapes that can even be layered using a top shape smaller than the one underneath. (Fig. 6) You could also cut the edges of the shapes with pinking shears or a rotary cutter with a wavy blade.

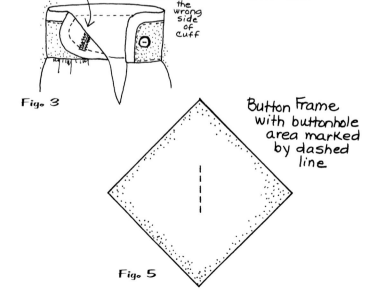

Fig. 3

Button Frame with buttonhole area marked by dashed line

Fig. 5

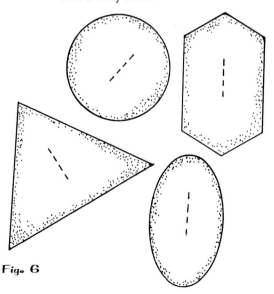

Fig. 6

Slip-Over Stole

Here's a movable embellishment for denim/chambray garments that you want to be able to wear plain as well as decorated. Make one or more versions of this stole to showcase unique fabrics, machine stitching, applique, or other trimming ideas. A stole can also be made reversible, with all four sides different. In the family picture on page 4, you'll see my sister Ruthie wearing the stole over a denim dress.

Slip-Over Stoles

Piece colorful Hoffman fabrics together or layer Ultrasuede over a printed design to trim stoles that slip over your head and decorate otherwise plain denim clothing. You'll see one of the stoles on my sister Ruthie in our family photo. She's always had a special way with plants, so I included a healthy ivy with the stoles I made for her.

Reversible Stole

Make the front and back of each stole different so you can wear them reversed. The beads are a fun feature whether you wear them on the back or the front.

Steps to Take:

1. Trace the stole pattern on page 74 and make a complete pattern by placing the pattern on folded paper where indicated. Cut a second complete paper pattern, pin the two together at the shoulder lines, and test the fit on yourself. (Fig. 1)

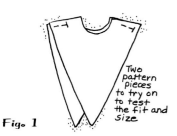

Fig. 1

Check the size and fit of the neck opening with the pattern on your front, back, and shoulders. Make any changes to the pattern before cutting out the fabrics for the stole. You may prefer to cut the stole pattern from scrap fabric for a more accurate fitting check. Note that the pattern pieces do not have seam allowances added. Plan to add 1/4" or more around all edges as you cut the pattern from fabric.

2. Cut four stole patterns from fabric. You can select four different fabrics or cut them all from the same fabric. Refer to the photo for ideas on piecing fabrics to form each side of the stole. This is the time to put your creativity to work and consider couching, applique, elegant machine stitching, beadwork, and on and on. Decorate each of the four stole pieces before assembling them.

3. To make the prairie points that form the buttonholes and also trim the stole front as pictured, cut 3" squares of fabric, fold them in half, then bring the folded corners down to the center of the unfolded edges. (Fig. 2) Sew these into the seams between pieces of fabric.

Prairie Points in Steps:

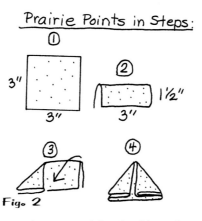

Fig. 2

4. At least one of the shoulders of the stole must open to allow for fabrics to be turned right side out. Decide if one or both shoulder seams will be open with button/buttonhole closures. If one shoulder will open, sew the shoulder seams of the opposite shoulder. Match the right sides of the stole front and back together and stitch across the shoulder seam. On the lining pieces, sew the matching shoulder seam. (Fig. 3)

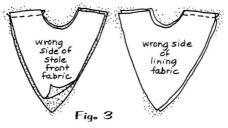

Fig. 3

5. Pin the prairie point piece or pieces to the open shoulder edges. With right sides of the fabrics together, pin the stole together. (Fig.4)

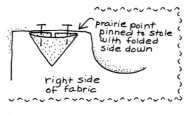

Fig. 4

Sew around the stole outer edges, stitching across the open shoulder edge with the prairie point(s) inserted, and leaving the opposite shoulder edge open. You'll be pulling the collar right side out through this opening. (Fig. 5)

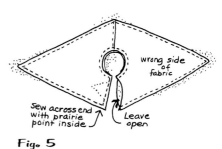

Fig. 5

6. Trim and clip the seam allowance, taking care to trim closely at the points on the collar front and back. Press the collar before turning it right side out. Press again and stitch the open shoulder edge closed.

7. Sew a buttonhole in the space between the folds of the prairie point. (Fig. 6)

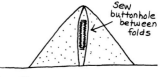

Fig. 6

Sew a button on the opposite shoulder area. Now your collar is ready to wear and enjoy. If you've made it reversible, you'll have lots of options for wearing this removable decoration.

~~~~~~

You can also change the shape and size of the collar to suit you and your garments. (Fig. 7) Add lace or piped edging and select interesting buttons for the closures at the shoulders. This is only the beginning of the possibilities for the slip-over stole.

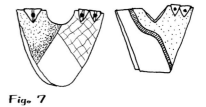

Fig. 7

Stole Pattern

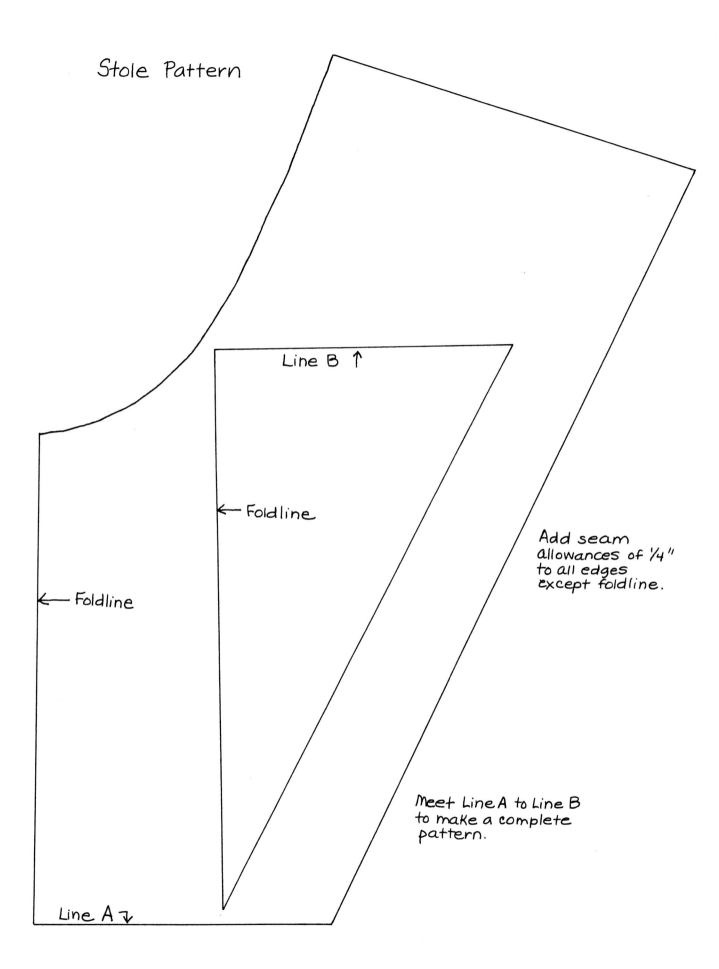

Line B ↑

← Foldline

← Foldline

Add seam allowances of ¼" to all edges except foldline.

Meet Line A to Line B to make a complete pattern.

Line A ↓

Seasonal Button-On Collar & Tuxedo Bib

Transform a plain shirt with a changeable system to coordinate with the seasons and holidays of the year. Make a wardrobe of collars and bibs to interchange and make them reversible for even more possibilities.

Supplies to Gather:

Denim shirt with collar and button front

1/2 yd. fabric for collar and bib

1/2 yd. lightweight fusible interfacing

Thread to match fabrics

5 small, flat buttons for collar and 3 buttons for bib

Steps to Take:

1. Make a collar pattern by laying the shirt collar flat and using the pattern tracing instructions in the Workshop section on page 121. Make the pattern 1/2" larger on the three sides of the collar and add a bottom extension the width of the shirt's collarstand. (Fig. 1)

Button-On Collars and Tuxedo Bibs
Change a denim shirt for holidays or seasons with a collection of collar covers and front bibs. Make each piece reversible for even more options. On the shirt you'll see the two-piece fall and Christmas set, and displayed below is the spring set.

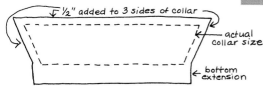

Fig. 1

(figure labels: ½" added to 3 sides of collar; actual collar size; bottom extension)

2. Cut two collars from fabric. Two different fabrics make the collar reversible. Apply lightweight interfacing to the wrong side of one of the collars. With right sides together, sew the collars together with a 1/4" seam allowance. Leave the bottom edge of the collar extension open. (Fig. 2) Turn the collar right side out and press. Turn under the open edges of the collar 1/4", press, and sew the opening closed.

Fig. 2

3. Select five small flat buttons for the collarstand. I chose clear buttons to blend with all fabric colors. Space them equidistant on the collar extension, mark the buttonhole spaces, and sew the buttonholes with thread to match the collar fabrics. (Fig. 3) Pin the collar extension to the shirt collarstand and mark the button locations to match the spacing of the buttonholes. Sew the buttons to the collarstand.

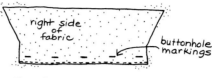

Fig. 3

4. Now it's time to make the tuxedo bib. Trace the pattern on page 78 and make a complete pattern by placing the pattern on folded paper. (Fig. 4)

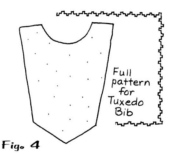

Fig. 4

Test the size and length by pinning the paper pattern on the shirt front and trying on the shirt. Pay attention to the bottom point and the fit over the bustline. Change the pattern to suit you and the shirt. You can also extend or shorten the length so the bottom buttonhole matches a button already on the shirt.

5. Cut two tuxedo bib shapes from fabric, adding a 1/4" seam allowance to all the edges. Use two different fabrics to make the bib reversible. Fuse lightweight interfacing to the wrong side of one of the bib fabrics if you wish to stabilize the fabric. With right sides of the fabrics together, sew around the bib with a 1/4" seam allowance, leaving an opening on one side for turning. (Fig. 5) Turn the bib right side out and press.

Ultrasuede Button-On Collar and Tuxedo Bib

This can be a no-sew project if you skip the applique on the bib. Use a wavy edge rotary cutter to cut the Ultrasuede collar and bib. Carefully cut buttonholes in each piece with a buttonhole cutter or small sharp scissors.

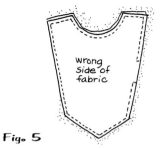

Fig. 5

6. Sew buttonholes at the shoulders and the bottom point of the bib. Sew buttons at the shirt shoulders and shirt front (if needed) to match the buttonholes. (Fig. 6)

Fig. 6

Ultrasuede is another fabric possibility for this project, as shown in the photo on the previous page. A single layer of the fabric will require no sewing and can be cut with a wavy edge rotary cutter. Buttonholes can then be cut with a single strike of a buttonhole cutter. Trim the fabrics by cutting holes with an eyelet punch or with applique.

Applique Pattern
for Ultrasuede Tuxedo Bib

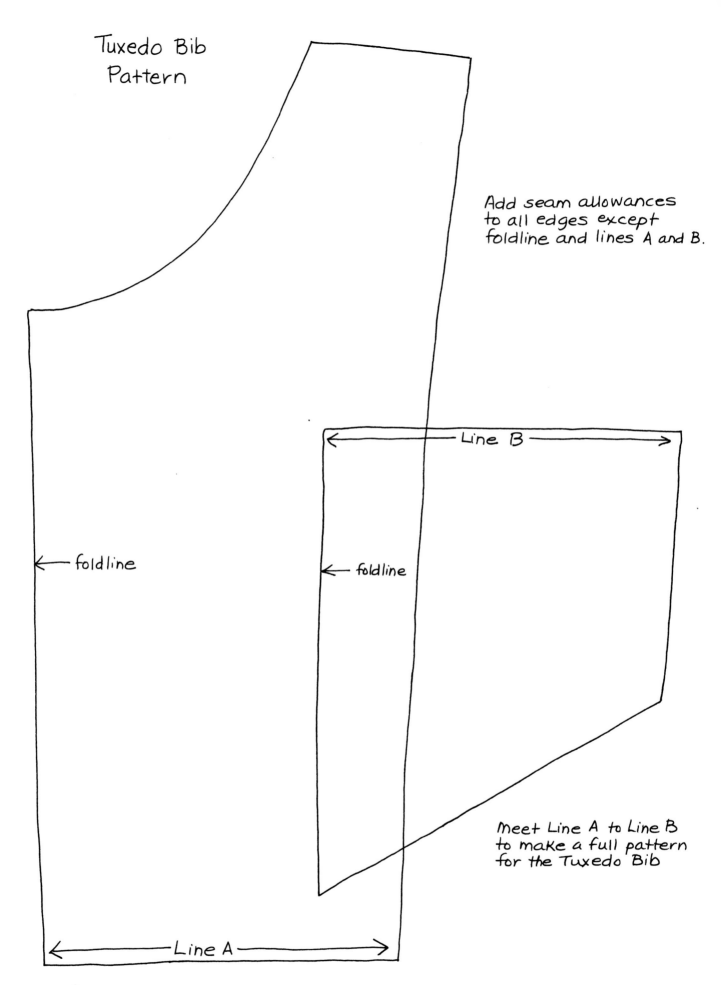

Tuxedo Bib
Pattern

Add seam allowances
to all edges except
foldline and lines A and B.

Line B

foldline

foldline

Meet Line A to Line B
to make a full pattern
for the Tuxedo Bib

Line A

PAINTING & STAMPING

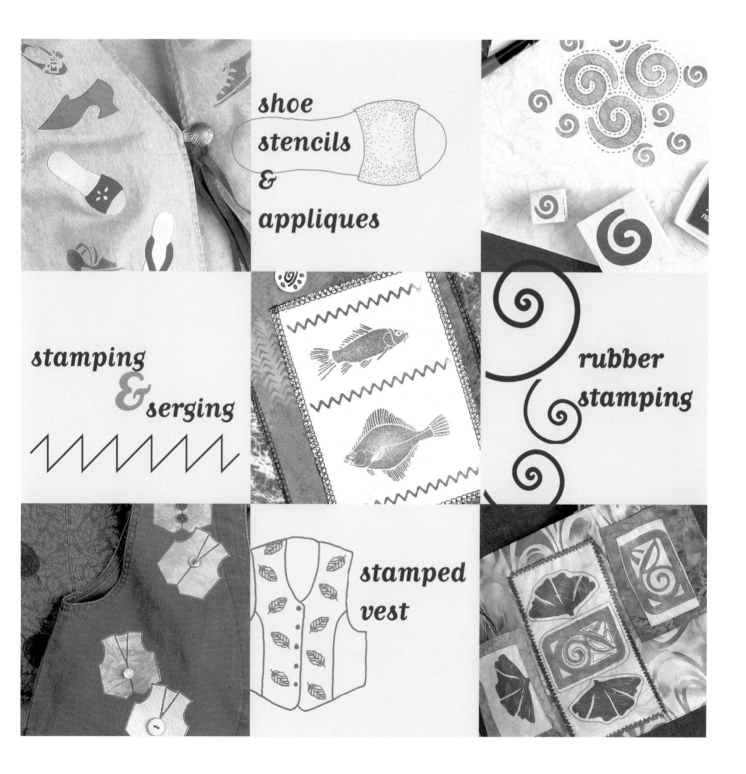

shoe
stencils
&
appliques

stamping
&
serging

rubber
stamping

stamped
vest

Shoe Stencils & Appliques

On a vest for a shoe aficionado, add a variety of shoe styles with both stenciling and applique techniques. The combination of paint and fabric adds contrast and special interest to an ordinary garment. The stencil package used for this project is Diane Ericson's "Shoes" stencils (see Resources). The shoe appliques are my designs and are made from Ultrasuede (find the patterns on page 82).

Shoe Theme Vest

Combine paint, fabric, and shoelaces to trim a plain vest. The shoe stencils are by Diane Ericson of ReVisions (see Resources) and the appliques are made from Ultrasuede. The shoelaces tied to the vest button add another dimension of trim. Don't forget to add your designer label to the garment as I did on the back neck facing. The vest is by Sunbelt.

Supplies to Gather:

Chambray vest or other chambray garment

Stencil, fabric paint, sponge applicator

Styrofoam plate or tray for pouring out paint

Paper and fabric for practicing stenciling

Paper towels

Cardboard or layers of paper to place inside garment before stenciling

Ultrasuede scraps for appliques

Fusible spray

Clear nylon thread

Lightweight tear-away stabilizer

Colored shoelaces for button trim

Steps to Take:

1. Choose a light colored garment for stenciling so dark colors show well on the fabric. If you decide to both stencil and applique on a garment, I recommend that you stencil first, then applique after the paint has dried. That way, if you goof with the stenciling, you can cover it up with an applique. (You wonder how I know this?)

2. Pour a small amount of paint on a Styrofoam plate. Work a sponge applicator into the paint, spreading it out onto the plate. (Fig. 1)

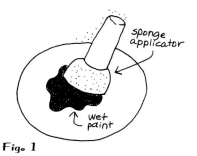

Fig. 1

Expert stencilers recommend a very small amount of paint on the applicator, so use the paper towels to remove excess paint. Practice by stenciling on paper or scraps of fabric and lightly pouncing the sponge applicator over the open sections of the stencil design. Stencil several copies of each design you plan to use, allow the paint to dry, then cut the stenciled paper or fabric apart so the designs can be used as patterns for planning the design layout on the vest.

3. Try on the vest to mark the bustline. Place the stenciled designs on the vest, along with paper copies of the appliques you plan to sew (applique patterns are on page 82). When you're pleased with the layout, pin the pieces to the vest. (Fig. 2)

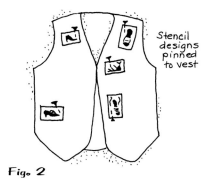

Fig. 2

4. On your work table, slide a piece of cardboard or several layers of paper inside the vest so the paint won't go through to the back of the garment. (Fig. 3) Even though you won't be soaking the fabric with paint as you stencil, it's a good idea to add a safety shield between the layers of the garment.

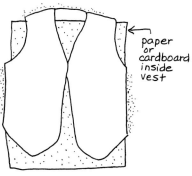

Fig. 3

5. Remove the pinned-on designs one at a time and carefully place the stencil in position. Apply the paint with the sponge applicator. You may want to lift a corner to see if the design is complete and dark enough. Then carefully lift off the stencil.

6. Allow the paint to dry for 24 hours (or more if the paint directions require it). Many fabric paints also require heat setting after the paint dries. Once these steps are complete, it's safe to add the appliques.

7. Trace the shoe applique designs on page 82. Cut the shoes from pieces of Ultrasuede and spray-fuse the wrong sides of the fabric. Place the

designs in position on the vest and add stabilizer to the wrong side of the garment beneath the design areas. Sew around the edges with clear nylon thread and the blanket stitch.

8. To add another shoe element to the vest, wrap and tie colorful shoelaces around the top vest button. (Fig. 4)

Fig. 4

Once you try stenciling on fabric and discover how easy it is to do, you'll enjoy trying it again. Test your ideas and brainstorms on scrap fabrics to gain confidence.

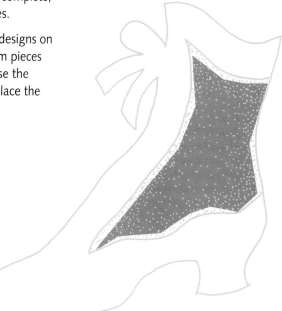

Shoe Applique Designs

Rubber Stamping for the Timid

If you worry about bad results from rubber stamping directly on a garment, try this method. Stamp designs on pieces of fabric then applique the stamped designs to clothing or accessories. This way, you can rubber stamp on loose pieces of fabric, save your collection of stamped designs, and later sew them as trim. It's also a way to use light and dark paint colors on dark denim items.

Supplies to Gather:

Denim apron or other garment

Rubber stamps

Fabric paint and sponge applicator or inked stamp pad

Paper and fabric for practice stamping

Paper towels, sponges, cotton swabs, and toothpicks for cleanup

Steps to Take:

1. As with any new project, practice is the best way to begin. Work on paper and fabric to get the feel of how to use and press on the stamp. Try different colors of fabric and consider using the underside for a more faded, softer background for stamps.

2. Work on a hard surface. I found that the bathroom counter was the right height for me to work and press on the rubber stamps. Apply the paint to the rubber stamp or press the stamp into the ink pad, then press firmly onto the paper or fabric swatch and lift it straight up. Play around - try stamping a second image over the first one either with a different stamp or a different color.

Rubber Stamping on Fabric Patches

Turn rubber stamping on fabric into unique appliques to trim an apron or other garment. Decorative stitching and fabric frames enhance the designs. These rubber stamps and paints are from ZimPrints. The cup and saucer are the pattern of my parents' wedding china - a lucky find at a garage sale.

3. To clean the stamps, press them on paper or paper towels to remove most of the ink. Then press them on a wet sponge and more paper towels. It's important to remove the paint from the rubber area. Use toothpicks and cotton swabs to clean the cracks and small indentations.

4. Allow the stamped image to dry on the fabric according to the instructions with the fabric paint or fabric paint pad. If heat setting is required, follow the instructions for that as soon as the paint is dry.

5. Now you're ready to do something with the stamped fabric pieces. The apron pictured was trimmed with three pieces of stamped fabric. The center piece with the coffee cup covers a seam in the apron, a place where it would be impossible to rubber stamp directly on the fabric. Yarn is also couched over the image to represent a drawstring tie. Each of the smaller pieces of coffee-bean-stamped fabric is sewn to the apron with decorative stitches over a second fabric frame.

It's fun to combine rubber stamping and sewing. Make and save a collection of stamped images on fabric for the day when you want an unusual accent for a denim garment.

Stamping Supplies

The possibilities for fabric stamping are endless! Here you'll see some of the stamps and products I've used and enjoyed, as displayed on a denim shirt stamped by Dana Bontrager with Pelle's stamps. On the left, the spiral stamps and design are by All Night Media stamps, the Fabrico stamp pad and pens are from Tsukineko, the fish stamp designs and white ink pad at the top are Pelle's stamps from Purrfection Artistic Wearables, and the coffee cup and ginkgo stamps are by ZimPrints. See Resources on page 126 to contact these companies.

Stamping & Serging

Even small rubber stamping samples can be used to create artwork to wear. The edges of two fabrics were serged before the work was assembled, and three buttons add extra spots of trim above the design.

Stamping and Serging

A stamped fish design becomes the focal point of a larger applique design on a jumper. The fish fabric piece and the orange fabric have serged edges for another dimension to the design. The stamp is by Pelle's (see Resources).

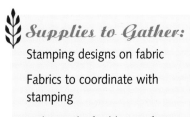

Supplies to Gather:

Stamping designs on fabric

Fabrics to coordinate with stamping

Lightweight fusible interfacing

3 buttons

Steps to Take:

1. Refer to the photo as a guideline or use the sizes shown in the illustration to determine the size of the three fabric pieces for this project. (Fig. 1)

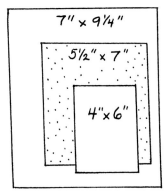

Fig. 1

2. Following the stamping instructions in Rubber Stamping for the Timid on page 83, complete the rubber stamping and allow the fabric to dry. If required, heat set the design, following the manufacturer's directions. On light-colored fabrics such as the design shown, fuse a piece of lightweight fusible interfacing to the back of the fabric to prevent shadowing of the darker fabrics beneath.

3. Serge the edges of the stamped fabric. Also serge the edges of the fabric to be placed beneath the stamping fabric. You can serge the edges of the third and largest piece as well, or turn under the edges, as I did on the jumper.

4. Assemble the entire piece and zigzag the top two serged fabrics to the third background fabric. For a hidden seam, use a wide zigzag stitch with thread to match the serger thread.

Sew the outline of the background fabric to the garment.

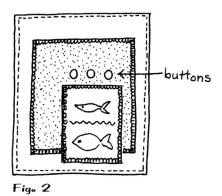

Fig. 2

5. Sew or pin on buttons to enhance your stamped design. (Fig. 2)

It pays to save your rubber stamping samples and trial runs. All by itself, the stamping piece featured on this project is not nearly as interesting as it has become with frames of additional fabrics, contrasting serged edges, and buttons.

Rubber Stamping on Pockets

Small rubber stamped images on yellow marbled fabric become pocket trim on the tote bag pictured. It pays to save all your fabric stamping experiments for projects like this.

Supplies to Gather:

Tote bag with plain front

Rubber stamped fabric swatches

Coordinating fabrics for pockets

Clear nylon thread

Rayon thread for embellishment stitching

1/4 yd. stabilizer.

Paper-backed fusible web or fusible spray

Steps to Take:

1. Plan the layout of the designs and sizes of the pockets. As shown, two small pockets overlap the large pocket on the front of the tote bag. The stamped designs are sewn off-center on all three of the pockets for an unusual effect. Cut the pocket fabrics, allowing seam allowances on all sides, and a wider seam allowance at the top edge. (Fig. 1)

Rubber Stamping on Pockets

Stamping samples become pocket applique trim on this tote bag. The rubber stamps and paints are by ZimPrints and the fabrics are by Hoffman (see Resources).

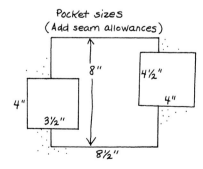

Pocket sizes
(Add seam allowances)

8"

4½"

4"

4"

3½"

8½"

Fig. 1

2. Start with the largest stamped image you have and plan to stitch it to the main or largest pocket on the tote bag. The example pictured is a three-part stamped design with decorative straight stitching outlining each of the shapes. (Fig. 2)

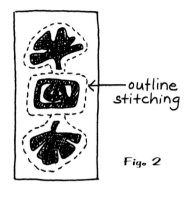

Fig. 2

outline stitching

Fold under and press the seam allowances of the pocket and the top edge. Turn under and machine stitch or fuse the top edge of the pocket. Use paper-backed fusible web or fusible spray to hold the stamped fabric in position on the pocket. Place a piece of stabilizer behind the pocket fabric and under the design area. Sew around the edge with a decorative stitch such as the "grass" stitch featured on the tote bag. (Fig. 3)

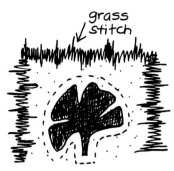

grass stitch

Fig. 3

3. Trim and assemble the two smaller pockets. Pin them to the large pocket. Sew the smaller pocket edges on top of the larger pocket, reinforcing the corners with back stitching. End the stitching 1/4" from the outside edge of the large pocket. (Fig. 4)

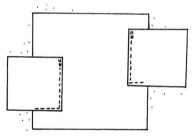

Fig. 4

4. Position the pocket unit on the tote bag and pin only the large pocket to the bag, folding back the smaller pockets over the main pocket. Sew around the edges of the main pocket and reinforce the upper corners. (Fig. 5) Sew the loose edges of the two smaller pockets to the tote bag, meeting the stitching you did previously to attach them to the main pocket.

Fold back small pockets

Fig. 5

Have fun carrying your decorated tote and storing your treasures in the pockets. Sew Velcro to the top opening of the main pocket so it won't gap open.

Dana Bontrager's Stamped Vests

"I found this printed denim vest and thought the leaf design in the denim would be greatly enhanced with a stamped leaf image. Since the fabric is somewhat dark, I decided to use a two-step process to stamp the design. This involves having two stamps that are designed to work together. One is a solid image and the other is the outline. By stamping one over the other, you can use different colors and also get a feeling of depth. You may want to make several test stampings on scrap fabric. Achieving good results with layered stamping takes a little practice, but once you get the hang of it, the results are exciting."

Dana Bontrager

BIRCH LEAF VEST

Supplies to Gather:

Denim vest

Pelle's Birch Stamp #2371 and Solid Birch #2372

Pelle's Textile Inks - Ultramarine Blue, Yellow Green

Pelle's blank stamp pad

Soft toothbrush and dishwashing liquid to clean stamps

Optional: chalk marker

Steps to Take:

1. Pre-wash the vest to remove any sizing. Sizing in fabrics and purchased clothing will limit the life of your stamped garment. Sizing acts as a barrier and prevents the paint from firmly adhering to the fibers. Over time, as the sizing washes away, so will your paint.

2. Textile paints and inks can easily seep through a garment. Be sure to protect your stamping surface in addition to the inside of the garment if you cannot work on a single layer. I use butcher paper to protect my work table. This paper is designed to keep leakage to a minimum.

Dana's Stamped Vests

Use Dana Bontrager's clever stamping techniques to add birch leaf trim and stamped vest appliques to plain denim vests. The stamps and inks are by Pelle's (see Resources).

3. Arrange your stamps and paints. The "rinsable" blank stamp pad allows you to work with two different colors of paint. This pad is designed to be used over and over simply by rinsing out one color and applying the next.

4. Plan your stamp locations on the garment and mark them lightly with a chalk marker or pin. I like random spacing. By pre-marking where you want the images to be, you will avoid an unbalanced finished project. (Fig.1)

Fig. 1

5. Apply Yellow Green textile ink to the stamp pad, spreading it evenly with a spatula or the back of a spoon. When ready, the pad will be squishy and wet, but the paint will be absorbed. It takes a little while, so have patience. Lightly tap the solid birch stamp up and down on the pad. Don't push down on the pad, as the stamp will become saturated. Check to see if the image is completely inked. If not, continue lightly tapping on the pad.

6. Hold the stamp over the area to be stamped. With one hand holding the stamp on the garment, push the fingers of your other hand on the mount to get a great impression. When fabric stamping, always stamp on a hard surface. Stamp solid birch images with Yellow Green. Allow to

dry. When you're finished with the solid stamping, rinse out the stamp pad and apply the second color, Ultramarine Blue.

7. You will now be stamping the outline birch leaf over the previous solid stamped image. Since you can see through the stamp, the job is so much easier! Ink the outline leaf and carefully place it over the stamped solid leaf image. Stamp over all previous solid stamped images. Don't worry if they're not exact. It looks more dimensional if it appears to be a double image. (Fig. 2)

Fig. 2

8. When you're finished stamping, clean the stamps thoroughly. A soft toothbrush and mild dishwashing detergent are best for cleaning detailed stamps.

9. Let the stamped images dry, then heat set them with a dry iron. Curing is necessary for all textile paints or inks. Allow your stamped fabric to dry thoroughly for 24 to 48 hours before washing. The longer you allow it to cure, the better the image will remain. Heat setting is recommended to keep the vibrancy of the colors and images after washings. Iron over your image with a dry iron at the hottest setting your fabric will withstand for 30 to 45 seconds.

STAMPED VEST APPLIQUES

"This purchased denim vest needed some color to liven it up. I decided to use my Appli-Stamp technique to add tiny versions of vests to the surface of the real one. Being able to stamp appliques makes the job go quickly. No more tedious tracing onto applique paper and design details are already there so you won't have to draw or stitch them in later."

Dana Bontrager

Supplies to Gather:

Denim vest

Pelle's Vest Stamp #2509

Pelle's Textile Ink - Ultramarine Blue

Pelle's Blank Stamp Pad

Variety of fabric scraps in different colors

Miscellaneous buttons in colors to match the fabrics

Steam-A-Seam Double Stick Fusible Bonding Web

Soft toothbrush and dishwashing liquid to clean stamp

Steps to Take:

1. Work on a hard surface for fabric stamping. Protect your stamping surface with butcher paper.

2. Collect and arrange the stamp, ink, and fabric scraps. You will need enough fabrics to make approximately 18 vest appliques. These can all be different, or as in the sample, you can make three each of six different colors. (Fig. 1)

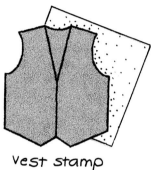

Vest stamp
Fig. 1

3. Apply ink to the stamp pad, spreading it evenly with a spatula or the back of a spoon. When ready, the pad will be squishy and wet but the paint will be absorbed. It takes a little while so have patience! Lightly tap the stamp up and down on the pad; don't push down on the stamp. Before pressing the stamp on fabric, check to see if the image is completely inked on the stamp. If not, tap it on the pad some more.

4. Line up the stamp over the area to be stamped. Hold the stamp with one hand and push the fingers of your other hand on the mount to get a great impression. Stamp the vest image on each fabric selected.

5. When the stamping is complete, clean the stamp thoroughly with a soft toothbrush and mild dishwashing detergent. Let the stamped images dry. Cut pieces of double stick fusible bonding web slightly larger than each vest image. Peel off one side of the paper backing and apply the web to the wrong side of the stamped fabric. Cut out the vest designs close to the stamped image.

6. Arrange the vest appliques on the vest front. The double stick fusible bonding web is great for this since it is repositionable. When you're satisfied with the arrangement, follow the manufacturer's directions to fuse the designs in place. (Fig. 2) Decorate the back of the vest with more little vests.

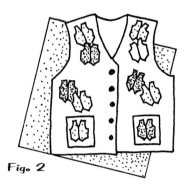

Fig. 2

7. Raid your button box for assorted small buttons to sew to the little vests. (Fig. 3)

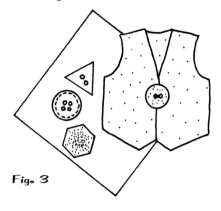

Fig. 3

This is a great way to add dimension to your project while using up a number of buttons. I also changed the closure buttons on my vest. It came with - you guessed it - ugly brown shirt buttons. I replaced them with crystal clear buttons I bought at an auction.

part 7

APPLIQUE INSPIRATIONS

Fractured Pictures

"Think Different," as the Macintosh Computer slogan suggests. Instead of using a square picture as an applique, cut it into pieces, like a broken piece of china, and applique it to a denim garment in its fractured state. Refer to the design in the photo to see how I cut a square design from printed fabric.

Supplies to Gather:

Denim jumper or garment with plain front

Printed fabric with design areas, preferably more than one so you can practice

Clear nylon thread

Double stick fusible bonding web (Steam A Seam 2 or AppliqEase)

1/2 yd. lightweight tear-away stabilizer

Wash-away marking pen

Steps to Take:

1. Apply double stick fusible bonding web, slightly larger than the design area, to the wrong side of the design you've chosen from the printed fabric.

2. Cut the design into sections or draw lines on the design with a wash-away marking pen to plan the cut lines in advance of cutting. On a square or rectangle, plan to cut two to three times on each 6" or longer side. This will help in reassembling the design with spaces between each piece and maintaining the same straight edges of the original piece of

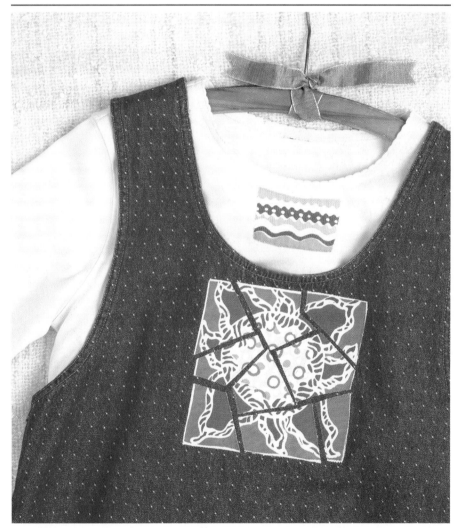

Fractured Pictures

Cut a design from printed fabric and cut it apart. Separate the pieces and sew them to a plain denim garment to create a mosaic effect. I added a small fractured piece to the knit shirt to be worn with the jumper.

fabric. (Fig. 1) If you want to do a practice cut first using extra fabric, do the cutting on a piece that doesn't have bonding web attached to it. If you like the way you cut the practice piece, trace the cut lines on another piece of the same fabric that you've treated with the bonding web. To duplicate the cutting pattern on my jumper, use the pattern on page 95.

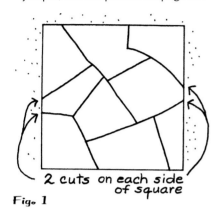

2 cuts on each side of square

Fig. 1

3. As you cut each piece from the design, place it in position on the garment. Leave a space of 1/8" to 1/4" between each piece. Arrange the pieces to achieve the look you want. You might prefer tilting out the corners of the design for more "movement." (Fig. 2) With the sticky backing on the pieces, you can move and rearrange the pieces many times. When they're in the right place, fuse the shapes in place on the garment.

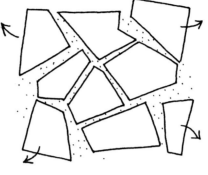

Fig. 2

4. Add a piece of stabilizer to the wrong side of the fabric before stitching. Use clear or smoke invisible nylon thread, depending on the colors in the applique fabric. Smoke nylon thread blends better with dark colors. Stitch with a zigzag stitch to secure each fractured piece of the design. Remove the stabilizer after stitching.

5. To add a coordinated touch to the t-shirt worn with the jumper, add a small section of the same printed fabric to trim the center front or sleeve edges. Now your outfit looks like it came from the ready-to-wear coordinates rack at your favorite department store.

A design block becomes much more interesting after a few cuts and spacing between the pieces. Consider this a sewing mosaic. Other treatments include adding a piece of tulle netting over the top of the pieced design to prevent the edges fraying and to subdue the color of the fabric. Stitch through the tulle and the design area to secure all the layers. Extra embellishments include buttons and couching to frame the design.

Before Cutting the Fabric Apart
Here you can see what the fabric started out as before I cut it into pieces.

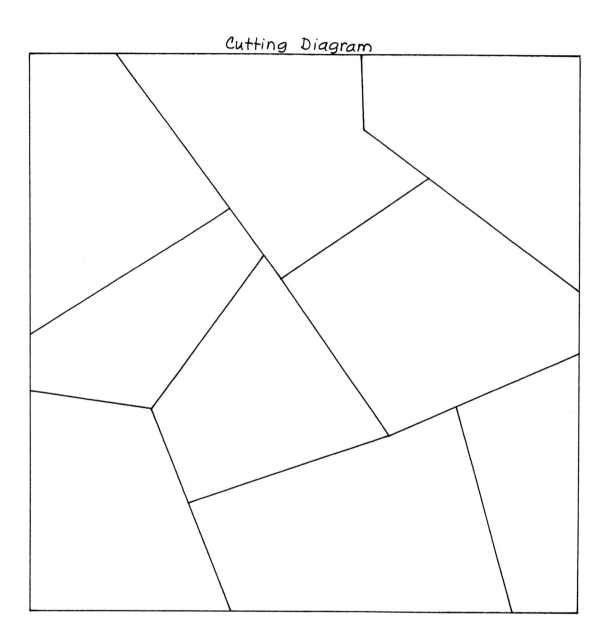

Cutting Diagram

Denim Shirt Inspired by the Buttons

Let the shape and colors of unusual buttons inspire an applique theme for a denim garment. As you'll notice on the shirt in the photo, an exact copy of the button isn't required for the applique shapes and colors.

Supplies to Gather:

Denim garment with button front

An interesting set or collection of buttons

Fabrics in colors to coordinate with the buttons

Clear nylon thread

Fusible spray or paper-backed fusible web

1/4 yd. stabilizer

Denim Shirt Trim Inspired by the Buttons

An unusual set of buttons designed by JJ Handworks (see Resources) gave me the idea to design appliques based on the button theme. Make sure the buttons you select will fit through the buttonholes of the garment and select a design shape and fabric colors that reinforce the spirit of the buttons.

Design on the back of the shirt.

Steps to Take:

1. Trace the button shape and enlarge it on a copy machine, or draw a larger, freehand version. The heart designs I created appear below in case you want to use them for a project of your own. Select the applique fabrics for their similarity to the button colors. If there are too many colors in the buttons, use only as many as you like. For my shirt, I used the idea of the striped lines crisscrossing through the button and created it as a single stripe flowing over each heart shape. (Fig. 1)

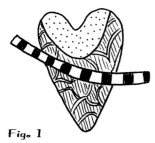

Fig. 1

2. Cut the applique shapes from fabric and apply them to the garment with temporary fusible spray or paper-backed fusible web. The heart shape I used has a green section layered over the purple fabric. See the basic applique instructions in the Workshop section on page 120. Sew the appliques to the garment with stabilizer pinned or otherwise attached to the wrong side of the garment.

3. The stripes added over the top are made from striped fabric with stripes 1/4" wide. Stripes cut across the grain of fabric can be "bent" to curve as they're sewn onto fabric. Cut the fabric strips 3/4" wide. Dampen them and fold and press 1/3 of the strip toward the wrong side of the fabric. Press in the opposite edge 1/3 of the way as well. (Fig. 2) You could also use a 1/4" bias tape maker for this project.

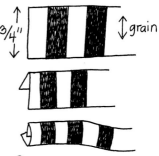

Fig. 2

4. Pin and sew the stripes on with clear nylon thread and a narrow zigzag stitch. Remove the stabilizer after all the stitching is done.

The heart shaped buttons I chose are created from polymer clay. See Resources on page 126 to contact JJ Handworks for a set of buttons of your own or sift through your button collection to find some unusual selections there. There's no reason you can't select five different buttons for this project.

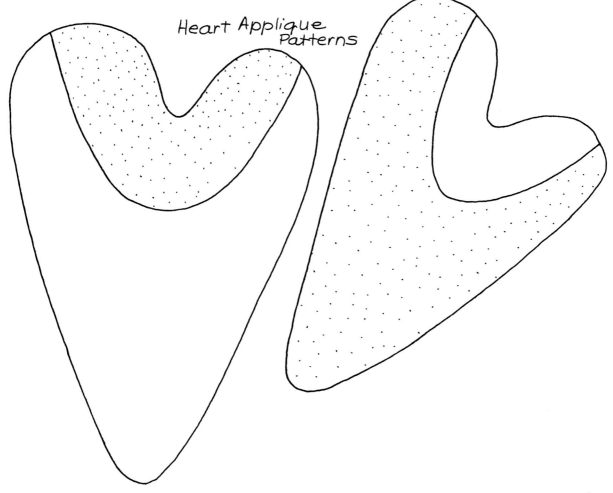

Heart Applique Patterns

Foundation Piecing Jacket Fronts

For the front of a very plain jacket, I chose a collection of Hoffman cotton prints and sewed them to a tear-away foundation, which became the jacket trim. The foundation panels are HTC's Fun-dation Possibility Panels and I used one rectangular crazy quilt block for both pieces of the jacket front. If you like this idea, consider using it on other clothing besides a jacket. I'm wearing the jacket in the photo with my sisters.

Foundation Pieced Jacket Trim
With foundation base piecing panels from HTC, I created the patchwork panel with Hoffman fabrics.

Supplies to Gather:

Denim jacket with plain front

Fun-dation Possibility Panels or foundation piecing base larger than area to be trimmed

Fabric selection for the piecing

Thread to coordinate with fabric colors, or clear nylon thread

Steps to Take:

1. Remove the buttons, if any, from the jacket front.

2. Check the foundation piecing base, positioning it on the garment to make sure it is larger than the areas to be covered. I built out the edges of the crazy quilt Possibility Panel so it would be large enough for the area on the jacket fronts. Select fabrics for each section of the design. (Fig. 1)

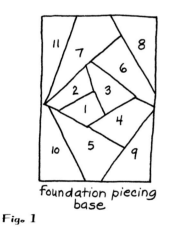

foundation piecing base

Fig. 1

3. Follow the manufacturer's directions for the foundation piecing base, placing and stitching the fabrics to the base in the order required by the numbers. Pin the fabric pieces right side down over the edge of the previous fabric stitched in place. Sew from the wrong side of the base, following the line drawn on the base. (Fig. 2) Use a short stitch length for a strong seam. Make sure to cut the fabric pieces large enough to cover each

section of the design completely. After sewing each section, flip it right side up to cover its portion of the base and press. Continue to sew on the next fabric piece until the entire foundation base is covered.

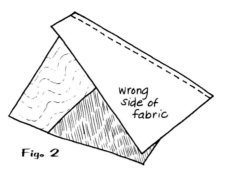

wrong side of fabric

Fig. 2

4. Tear away the backing or base and press the panel of fabrics you've created.

5. For the jacket front panels, I cut the Possibility Panel foundation piece in half lengthwise. Each piece was slightly larger than each side of the jacket area to be covered.

Pin each pieced panel to the jacket front, pinning in the center first and extending the pinning toward the edges. Turn under and pin the fabric edges to line up with the jacket neckline, shoulder area, sides, and bottom edges. (Fig. 3) For curved edges such as the neckline, it may help to trim and clip the seam allowance as you turn it under.

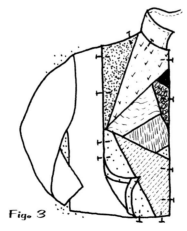

Fig. 3

6. After topstitching the turned-under edges in place all around both jacket fronts, press the pieced areas.

7. Now it's time to remake the buttonholes that you've covered with fabric (or leave the jacket without buttonholes, if you prefer an open garment). Restitch the buttonholes from the wrong side of the jacket with a narrow zigzag stitch. (Fig. 4) Cut the buttonholes open, also from the wrong side. Sew the original or different buttons on the other side of the jacket, making sure the buttons will fit the buttonholes. I chose five different gold buttons from my collection.

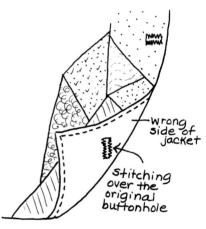

wrong side of jacket

Stitching over the original buttonhole

Fig. 4

Expand on the foundation piecing idea by drawing your own piecing arrangements on lightweight tear-away stabilizer. In this way, you can piece a new layer for the collar or cuffs of the jacket. You could also make or cover pockets with foundation-pieced creations.

Geometrics for Men

For "casual Fridays" at the office, a denim shirt with a collection of denim shapes becomes more than ordinary. Use the shapes to cover up a logo you no longer want to advertise or even a stain. This small design idea works for men or women.

Geometrics for Men
Combine denim variety fabrics in a simple applique design over the shirt pocket on a man's shirt. I tested the idea and design on my husband Barry. He said he'd wear it. That's an important question to ask before you sew! The shirt is by Sunbelt.

Supplies to Gather:

Denim shirt

Small pieces of different denim fabrics

Threads to match fabrics

Small piece of paper-backed fusible web

Small piece of stabilizer for beneath design area

Chalk marker

Steps to Take:

1. Trace the geometric pattern onto paper-backed fusible web. (The design appears in reverse to save you time in tracing.) Fuse each of the shapes onto the wrong side of the chosen fabrics and cut them out. For

color variety, look at the back side of denims to find a lighter shade. On the shirt pictured, the top gray shape is the wrong side of a piece of black denim.

2. Peel the paper backing off each shape and arrange them in the pattern shown, or make up your own arrangement. Set aside the long horizontal bar and fuse on the three remaining shapes. (Fig. 1)

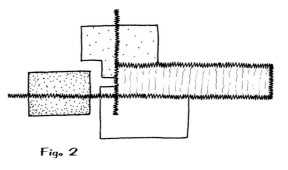

Fig. 2

Instead of the usual monogram, use the same or a smaller version of the geometric arrangement to trim the cuff. Another possibility for a shirt for the office is an overlapped arrangement of small argyle shapes, as illustrated. (Fig. 3)

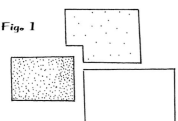

Fig. 1

Fuse and sew these shapes first.

Place a piece of stabilizer beneath the design area on the wrong side of the shirt. Sew around each of the three shapes with a satin stitch.

3. Fuse the long bar shape in place. With a chalk marker, draw the extension lines to be stitched from the ends of the bar. With thread to match the bar, satin stitch around the shape and onto the extended lines. (Fig. 2) Remove the stabilizer.

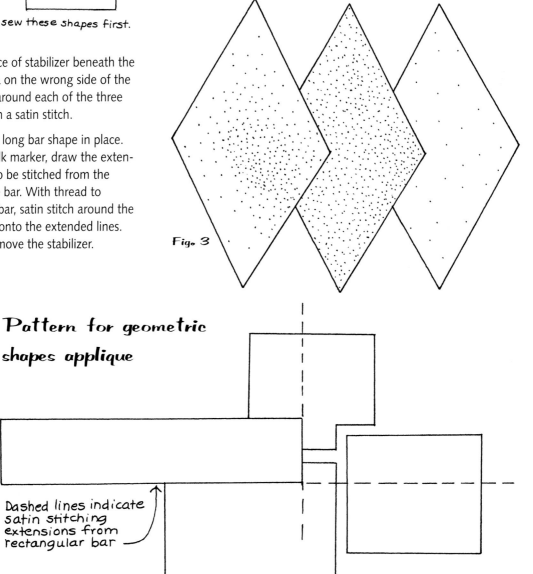

Fig. 3

Pattern for geometric shapes applique

Dashed lines indicate satin stitching extensions from rectangular bar

Nature Shirt

Nature designs are on display in a four-square pattern on a denim shirt. The shirt I chose doesn't have front pockets, so there's more room to decorate. Prominent decorative stitching frames the designs and trims the collar and cuffs.

Nature Shirt

Stitch a square area as borders for four nature theme appliques. I chose a feather stitch and Jeans Thread by YLI for this shirt.

Supplies to Gather:

Denim shirt with plain front

Fabrics for appliques - I chose Ultrasuede

Thread to match fabrics or clear nylon thread

Jeans Thread by YLI for topstitching

Topstitch needle, size 90 or 100

String or yarn for design planning

Fusible spray

1/2 yd. tear-away stabilizer

Steps to Take:

1. Trace the four nature applique designs on page 104 and cut them out of paper.

2. With pieces of string or yarn to mark the decorative stitching lines, plan the four-square design layout. To avoid placing the designs directly on the bustline, try on the shirt and mark the bustline. Does your shirt have a sewn-on front placket or a plain front, as my shirt in the photo has? If it has a placket, measure 4-1/2" on each side of the sewn-on placket and place the vertical strings along both sides. If it has a plain front, measure 4-1/2" from the button centers to determine the vertical borders of the design area and lay the string. (Fig. 1)

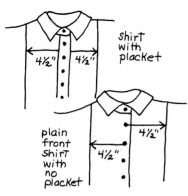

Fig. 1

Place the four paper designs within the vertical lines and lay two pieces of string to form the horizontal borders of the squares. (Fig. 2)

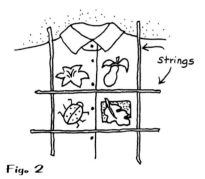

Fig. 2

Adjust the strings if necessary to allow enough space for each of the applique designs. Mark the lines of the frame design with a ruler and a chalk marker or wash-away marking pen. Remove the strings.

3. Cut and pin pieces of tear-away stabilizer on the wrong side of both shirt fronts. Make sure the stabilizer is under the areas of decorative stitching as well as the appliques.

4. Cut the applique designs from fabric, spray the wrong sides with temporary fusible spray, and attach them to the square areas. You could also trace the designs onto paper-backed fusible web and fuse them to

fabric to create a fuse-on applique shape. Cut small circles in the red body of the ladybug and place black fabric beneath, extending it to form the ladybug head. Position the pieces of each design within the frame lines on the shirt.

5. Sew the designs to the shirt with a small zigzag stitch, a buttonhole stitch, or satin stitches. (Fig. 3)

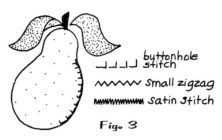

Fig. 3

Add the stitched details to the tiger lily flower and the ladybug. Sew a straight line with matching thread down the center of the oak leaf.

6. Redraw the decorative stitching frame lines on the shirt to make sure they are visible.

7. Thread the machine with Jeans Thread and use a topstitch needle. Practice with decorative stitches on scrap fabric with stabilizer beneath. I chose a feather stitch for my shirt. (Fig. 4)

Fig. 4

The Jeans Thread creates a very noticeable and dense stitch on garments. Sew slowly as you practice and select different stitches. You may need to loosen the sewing machine's top tension.

8. Stitch the frame lines drawn on the shirt front. Draw lines 1/2" from the edges of the cuffs and the collar to guide the decorative stitching in those areas.(Fig. 5) Pull the top thread to the wrong side of the garment and knot with the bobbin thread.

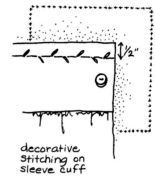

decorative Stitching on sleeve cuff

Fig. 5

9. The last step is to change the buttons of the shirt.

The four designs featured on the shirt are also featured on an embroidery/applique card I designed for Cactus Punch. The card will allow you to create the designs automatically with an embroidery unit on a sewing machine. See Mary's Productions in Resources on page 126.

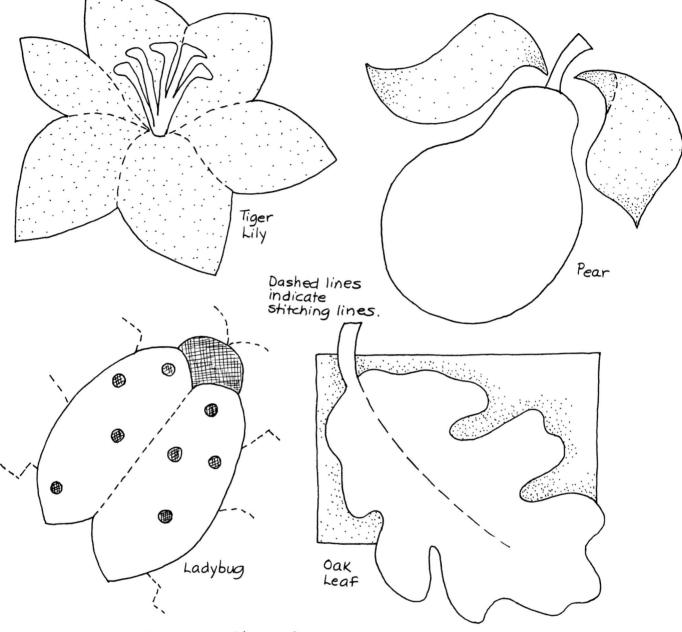

Tiger
Lily

Pear

Dashed lines
indicate
stitching lines.

Ladybug

Oak
Leaf

Nature Shirt Applique Patterns

Charmed Jumper

In the style of charm quilts that are assembled from a collection of small squares of fabric, this design on a jumper front features a variety of fabrics with extra trim added when the stitching was completed. Here's an opportunity to feature some favorite fabrics from your stash.

Supplies to Gather:

Denim jumper

Small pieces of fabric for cutting charm squares - I used 15

Quilting template plastic for cutting out pattern

Wash-away marking pen or chalk marker

Fusible spray

1/2 yd. stabilizer

Jeans Thread and size 100 topstitch needle

Optional: buttons and extra trim pieces

Charmed Jumper

Two-inch squares of Hoffman fabrics form a quilt-like design on this jumper top. Extra texture comes from two squares of chenille denim squares (see if you can find them) and a button, fabric yo-yo, and a small crocheted flower. The yo-yo and flower are from Wimpole Street Creations (see Resources).

Steps to Take:

1. The charm squares featured on the jumper started out as 2" squares. Cut out a 2" square template from quilting template plastic. This is the easiest and fastest way to position and cut the squares and you can also see through the plastic to position the square correctly. Trace the template on all the fabrics with a wash-away marking pen or chalk marker. Cut out the squares. For two of the squares on the jumper, I used pieces of chenille denim I created in experimenting with the technique. See the directions on page 38. (Fig. 1)

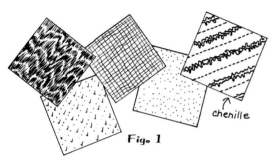

Fig. 1

chenille

2. Turn under the edges about 1/8" and press. Arrange the squares on the garment to plan your design. I placed the squares 1/4" apart on the jumper, but you can place them any distance apart. Then, one at a time, spray the wrong side of each square with fusible spray and place it back in the arrangement. Pin each square in place to keep all the squares in position, especially during the sewing and shifting around of the garment. Pin stabilizer to the wrong side of the garment beneath the design area. (Fig. 2)

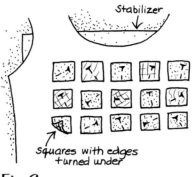

Stabilizer

Squares with edges turned under

Fig. 2

3. Thread the machine with Jeans Thread and use a topstitching needle, size 100. I chose a gold color to contrast with the squares and match the stitching on the jumper. Use standard sewing thread in the bobbin. Loosen the top tension. Select the blanket stitch and sew on scrap fabrics to test the stitching before working on the garment. Remember to sew slowly.

4. Sew around each of the squares with the Jeans Thread and blanket stitch. (Fig. 3)

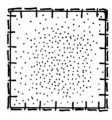

Fig. 3

Pull the top threads to the back of the garment and tie a knot. The chenille squares were stitched on with clear nylon thread and a zigzag stitch. Though I tried to pin and sew carefully, I found that some of the squares are a little crooked or not perfectly square. It's okay - it may even make the design a little more interesting.

5. Add the extra trims you want. I chose a shank button, cloth yo-yo, and a small crocheted flower. If you're not sure you'll always want them as part of the design, pin them on the garment with a "golden metallic fastener," a stylish way to refer to safety pins!

If you want to add another collection of charmed squares, look to the hemline area of the jumper, the end of a sleeve, or the back of the same garment.

Japanese Fans

Here's applique with an extra detail: The edges of the fans are defined by fusible bias tape. I chose black for this garment, but many other colors of this time-saving product are available, including metallic shades. It's a little like using packaged cake mixes to save time in the kitchen; pre-made bias tape with a fusible backing saves lots of time and energy... so we have more time to sew more things!

Japanese Fan Appliques

Choose Japanese theme fabrics and black fusible bias tape to assemble the fans shown on this denim top.

Supplies to Gather:

Denim garment with plain front or back

Fusible bias tape

Fabrics for centers of fans

9" square of paper-backed fusible web

Thread to match the bias tape

Optional: double needle size 4.0

Steps to Take:

1. When selecting fabrics for the fan centers, examine your stash for Japanese prints or kimono scraps. I also used a piece of fabric from a hanky left over from the Hanky Corner Jumper project on page 61.

2. To duplicate the design in the photo, use the pattern below to cut the three different-sized fan patterns out of paper. Trace the shapes onto paper-backed fusible web. Fuse each shape to a different fabric, cut out the fan shapes, then remove the paper backing.

3. Plan the position of the fans on the garment. Allow space between each one for the bias tape edging and extensions. Fuse the three shapes in place. (Fig. 1)

4. Cut and fuse the bias tape over the two curved edges of the fans. Sew the two edges of each strip in place with two straight seams, or use the 4.0 double needle and a straight stitch to secure each strip of bias tape in one step. (Fig. 2)

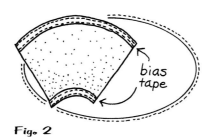

Fig. 2

5. Cut and fuse strips of bias over the straight sides of the fans and extend them so they intersect, forming the fan handle. (Fig. 3) Turn under the raw edges on each end of the strips.

Sew in place, sewing again on both sides of the bias tape.

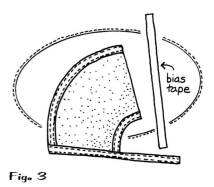

Fig. 3

Sew fans on the front, back, or sides of a garment. Other ideas for the fan centers include stitching samplers, machine embroidery designs, or Seminole piecing.

Fig. 1

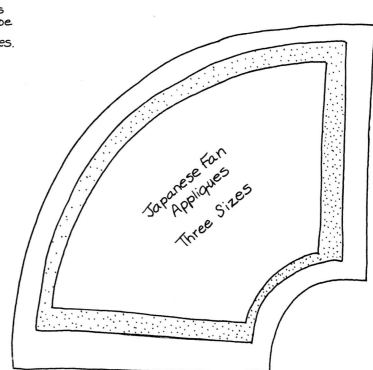

Dashed lines indicate extensions of bias tape to form fan handles.

Japanese Fan Appliqués Three Sizes

Indigo Patchwork

Start this shirt project with a question: What will you wear with the shirt? My plan was to wear the shirt pictured with black pants or a skirt, so I used several patches of black fabric, both on the front and the back, and stitched the patches with black thread. It was fun to assemble a selection of fabrics, ribbons, and trims to embellish an ordinary chambray shirt.

Supplies to Gather:

Denim or chambray shirt

Fabric collection - small pieces are adequate

Assorted ribbons and trims

Clear nylon thread

Thread to match or contrast with chosen fabrics

Paper-backed fusible web or fusible spray

1 yd. tear-away stabilizer

Steps to Take:

1. Many denim and chambray shirts have one or two front pockets, and for this project, these pockets should be removed. You'll see in the photo that I saved the pocket, added ribbon trim and later sewed it back to the opposite shirt front of the garment.

2. The decorated placket cover is a unique feature of this shirt project. It hides very ordinary but functioning buttons and buttonholes. You can see examples of the buttons covered by the placket toward the bottom of the shirt. The bottom edge of the placket cover should be located between two buttonholes or extended to the bottom of the shirt to cover all the buttons and buttonholes. I chose to sew mine just long enough to cover the area in view when the shirt is tucked into a skirt or pants.

Indigo Patchwork Shirt
Squares and pieces of fabrics are artfully arranged on the front and back of a chambray shirt. Select a color theme before you begin cutting fabrics. Other small trims such as a ribbon rose from C.M. Offray are incorporated in the shirt's design.

3. The placket cover can be any width you choose. For the shirt pictured, the placket cover was cut 4" wide and folded in half. The folded edge extends 1/4" beyond the actual shirt placket. (Fig. 1)

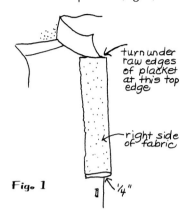

Fig. 1

Sew the placket lengthwise, wrong sides together, to the shirt front 1/4" from the raw edges. Then sew the braid or trim over the raw edges and the seam. This is a very quick way to cover and improve a shirt front. (Fig. 2) Naturally, you could add more features or trim to it if you want to get creative.

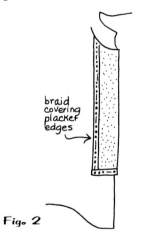

braid covering placket edges

Fig. 2

4. Next, plan the patchwork. Work first with the fabrics you want to be most prominent on the shirt. Cut those patches larger and position them first. Add smaller patches or rectangles of other fabrics with their edges over or under the larger patches. Experiment with pieces of ribbon and trims. A short piece of my mother-in-law's hand-crocheted trim

was chosen to cross the right shirt front. Buttons, ribbon roses, and other small trims could be pinned into place after the stitching is done, if you're not sure you want to attach them permanently. Arrange patches on the back of the shirt also. The illustration includes the measurements of all the patches I used on the shirt front pictured. (Fig.3) All patches have raw edges, but you could plan to turn under the edges before sewing.

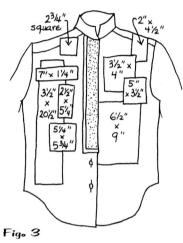

Fig. 3

5. After the patchwork layout is planned, apply paper-backed fusible web or fusible spray to the back of each piece. Add stabilizer to the shirt fronts and the back. Start with the patches that are underneath others and sew them on the shirt first. Use a satin or other decorative stitch. Then sew the overlapping patches.

6. Add a band of fabric to the center of the collar for an area of interest there. Measure the length of the collar and cut a piece of fabric to that length with 1/4" seam allowances on all sides. Turn under and press the seam allowances, pin the piece to the collar, and sew it on. (Fig. 4)

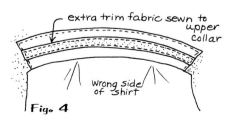

extra trim fabric sewn to upper collar

wrong side of shirt

Fig. 4

7. Now, about the cuffs... It's smart to wrap fabric around the cuff edges for color and for extra durability. I'm allergic to sewing the same fabric on both cuffs, so you'll notice I've chosen two different cuff edge covering fabrics that are repeated elsewhere on the shirt. Cut fabric strips 1" wide and slightly longer than the cuff edge. Press under one long edge and sew the opposite raw edge inside the cuff, right side of fabric to wrong side of cuff. (Fig. 5)

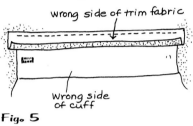

wrong side of trim fabric

wrong side of cuff

Fig. 5

Wrap the fabric over the cuff edge and pin the pressed edge to the cuff. Turn in the fabric at the cuff ends to meet the cuff edges. Sew in place. (Fig. 6) The cuff buttons have also been changed, for the better, I think!

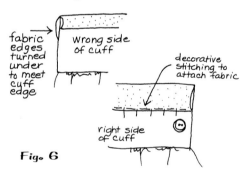

fabric edges turned under to meet cuff edge

wrong side of cuff

decorative stitching to attach fabric

right side of cuff

Fig. 6

When you complete this shirt creation, you will have a unique wearable not available in any store. After all, that's one reason we sew, isn't it?

Overlapping Bands

Two overlapping fabric bands are sewn around the neckline of this chambray shirt and open in the front. Choose four unique buttons, two for the front buttonholes and two more for the back, to add decorative interest.

Supplies to Gather:

Chambray shirt

1/2 yd. each of two coordinating fabrics

4 buttons

Chalk marker

2 small pieces of Ultrasuede for sewing under back buttons

Optional: lightweight fusible interfacing

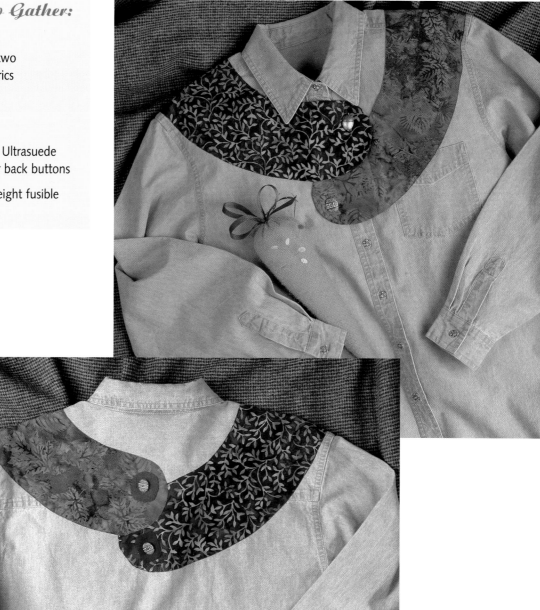

Overlapping Bands
Sew two fabric semicircles around a shirt yoke to frame your face and charming smile! The bands are buttoned to the shirt front and overlap in the back. The fabrics are by Hoffman.

Steps to Take:

1. Make a complete band pattern from the two pattern pieces on page 113. Trace two copies of piece A and one copy of piece B. Cut out the two pieces and tape them together as illustrated. (Fig. 1) Make a second complete band pattern by tracing the pattern you taped together. Mark the two C lines on the second copy.

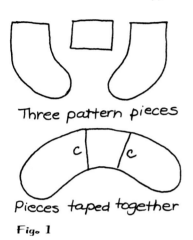

Three pattern pieces

Pieces taped together

Fig. 1

2. Try on the shirt with the pattern pieces to test the fit and to see how they will overlap on the front and back. The ends of the two pattern pieces should cross the placket area in the front and meet in the back. Refer to the photos to see how the bands connect. Adjust the pattern pieces at the pattern joining lines or change the width to fit the shirt you are decorating.

3. Cut the pattern piece from two different fabrics and mark the C lines on the right side of the fabric with a chalk marker. One of these lines on each band will meet the shirt yoke line. Note that the shorter portion of the band extends from the yoke line on the left side of the shirt and the longer portion is aligned with the yoke line on the right band of the pictured shirt. (Fig. 2)

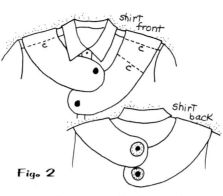

shirt front

shirt back

Fig. 2

4. Cut lining pieces for the two front overlapping ends of the fabric bands. Add lightweight fusible interfacing to the lining if you want to support the buttonhole that will be stitched through the overlapped bands. (Fig. 3)

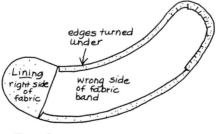

Lining Sections

interfacing on wrong side

Fig. 3

5. Sew the linings to the front ends with the right sides of the fabric facing and using 1/4" seam allowances. Turn the ends right side out and press. Turn under and press 1/4" seam allowances around the rest of each band. (Fig. 4)

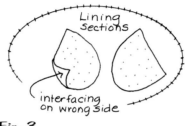

edges turned under

Lining right side of fabric

wrong side of fabric band

Fig. 4

6. Place and pin the two bands on the shirt, making sure the lined ends are on the front and the pattern joining lines (C lines) are lined up at the yoke lines. Try the shirt on and adjust the fit of the bands on the front and back, if necessary.

7. Begin sewing 2" to 3" from the front placket edges on each band and sew all around each band. (Fig. 5)

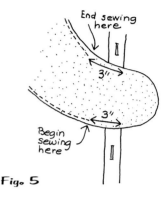

End sewing here

3"

3"

Begin sewing here

Fig. 5

8. Sew buttonholes at the lined ends of the bands. Sew or pin buttons to the shirt front. On the back of the bands, sew two more buttons or first sew circles of Ultrasuede on the curved ends of the bands and then sew or pin buttons in the center of the Ultrasuede. Refer to the photo for a placement suggestion.

〰〰〰〰〰〰〰〰〰〰〰〰〰〰〰〰〰〰〰〰

The lower band on the shirt front covers a portion of the shirt pocket. I chose to ignore the pocket when I sewed it in place. It's easier than trying to remove the pocket and finding a different color of fabric under the pocket or dealing with the holes left by removing it.

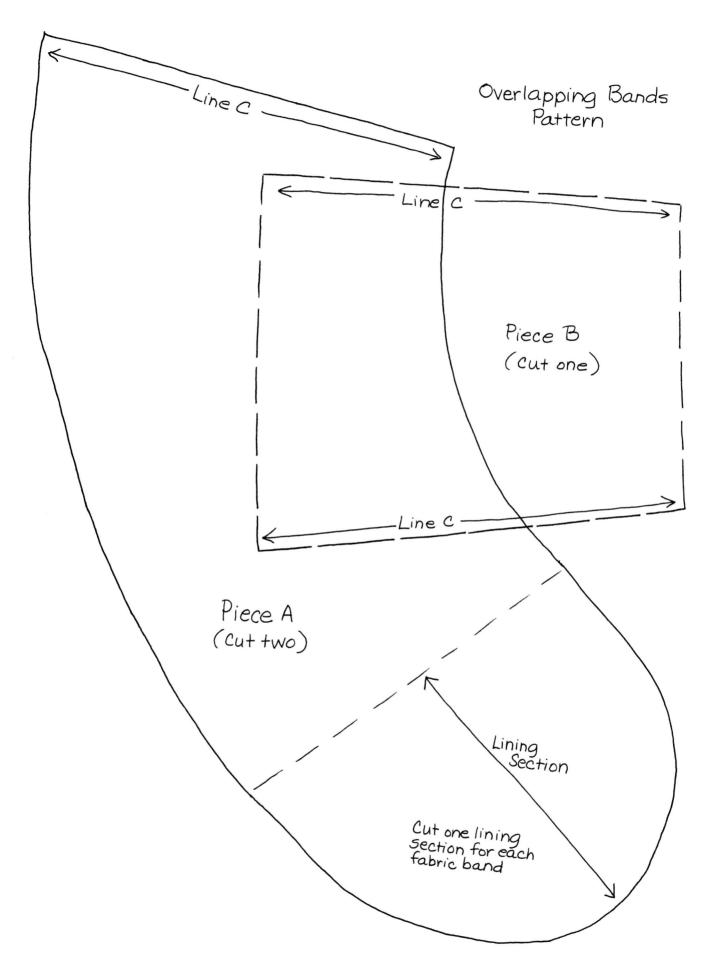

Overlapping Bands
Pattern

Line C

Line C

Piece B
(cut one)

Line C

Piece A
(cut two)

Lining
Section

Cut one lining
section for each
fabric band

doily vest from a
denim shirt

teddy bear jeans
from a shirt

Doily Vest from a Denim Shirt

Salvage a faded or stained denim shirt from your closet or a rummage sale. Then collect some doilies. Remove the shirt's sleeves, collar, and collarstand, and turn it into an unusual lace covered vest. Make sure the shirt is large enough to fit over other clothing. You're sure to hear many compliments when wearing this vest.

Supplies to Gather:

Denim shirt to cut apart

Doilies or pieces of lace fabric to cover the shirt fronts and back

6 yards of 1" wide lace for binding vest edges

Fusible spray

Washable marking pen or colored chalk marker

3 yds. of wide bridal tulle in a color of your choice

Bobbin thread to blend with denim color

Top thread to match doilies or contrast with denim

Long flower head pins

Steps to Take:

1. When you've chosen your shirt for this project, check to see that it fits loosely over other clothing, especially in the hip area. Pin doilies over the top and experiment with different colors of bridal tulle to see the effect of the colors over the doilies and denim. The differences will be subtle, but you might find a color preference.

2. Use a straight stitch to sew around the shirt neckline right below the

Doily Covered Vest

Transform a denim shirt into a feminine, lace covered vest. It's a great way to recycle a doily or lace fabric collection and also a denim shirt with stains or tears.

collarstand. After that, it's safe to cut off the collar and collarstand above the staystitching, and the neckline won't become distorted or mis-shapen. (Fig. 1)

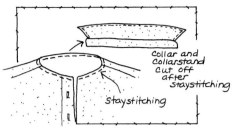

Fig. 1

3. Cut open the side seams of the shirt. Cut off the sleeves. Remove the buttons from the shirt front. You can remove the pockets if you wish, but there's no need to, since they will be covered by doilies.

Cutting Up a Denim Shirt
Cut off the collarstand and collar (after understitching), the sleeves, buttons, and pocket flaps. Open the side seams. Now you're ready to plan the doily layout.

4. If there is a pleat in the back of the shirt, stitch down the folds, then press the shirt. (Fig. 2)

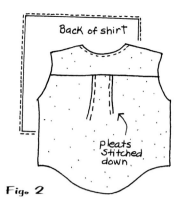

Back of shirt

pleats stitched down

Fig. 2

5. Lay the shirt flat on a table or the floor with newspaper or other disposable paper underneath. (Fig. 3)

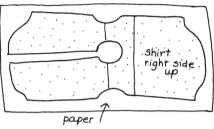

Shirt right side up

paper

Fig. 3

Plan the layout of the doilies and lace pieces. Start by placing a larger doily over the neck area. It can be centered carefully or placed off-center. (Fig. 4) Trim away pieces of doilies that extend over the vest edges and use those pieces in other areas of the vest. You can either overlap the doilies or leave gaps and fill the gaps with pieces of lace fabric or wide lace trim.

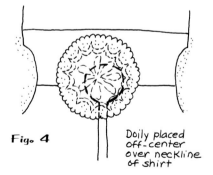

Fig. 4

Doily placed off-center over neckline of shirt

6. After determining the doily layout and covering all the areas of the vest fronts and back, move each doily and lace piece one at a time to an-

other piece of newspaper. Spray the back of each doily with fusible spray, then put it back in its place on the vest before removing the next doily.

7. Spray with fusible spray over the doily covered vest and lay the bridal tulle over the top. (Fig. 5)

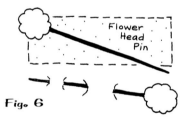

paper   tulle

Fig. 5

Cut the tulle so that it extends generously beyond the vest edges. To better secure all three layers together, pin the tulle in place on the vest fronts and back. I used flower head pins, which are easy to see and can be pinned in and out twice so they stay in place. (Fig. 6)

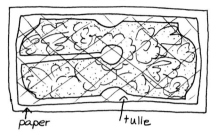

Flower Head Pin

Fig. 6

8. Mark two intersecting perpendicular lines on the vest. (Fig. 7)

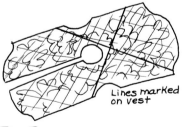

Lines marked on vest

Fig. 7

Use a washable marking pen or colored chalk marker, making sure the lines can be easily seen. Roll up and pin the vest edges so one of the lines is exposed. (Fig. 8)

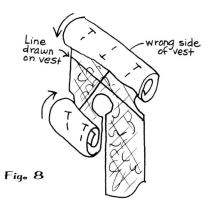

Fig. 8

9. Prepare to sew with a size 90 needle. Test different top thread colors in the vest seam areas. Thread colors can match or contrast with the doilies and tulle. For the vest pictured, I used blue thread as the top thread. Bobbin thread that matches the shirt color will produce inside seams that blend with the shirt.

10. Select a straight or decorative stitch and sew along the intersecting lines marked on the vest. Keep the loose edges of the vest rolled up as much as possible to prevent the pins from coming out and for easier handling of the project. Stitch rows parallel to the two you marked, using the quilting bar on the sewing machine to guide you. I chose to stitch with 1-1/2" between the rows. (Fig. 9) Sew the stitching lines, following both perpendicular rows on the vest so you have a quilted effect with the stitches holding the three layers in place. Sew slowly, especially through overlapping layers of doilies.

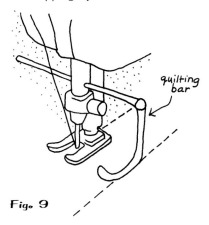

Fig. 9

11. After sewing the lines on the vest fronts and back, straight stitch around the edges of the entire piece, stitching on the garment side to secure all layers together. Trim away excess lace and tulle. (Fig. 10)

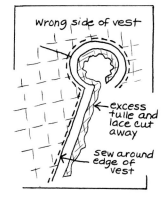

Fig. 10

12. Test the vest fit by pinning the side seams together and trying it on. Check the shoulders and trim them if they are too wide. You can also round out the corners at the neckline and vest fronts. (Fig. 11)

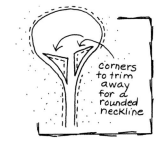

Fig. 11

Remove the pins and press the vest, pressing from the wrong side of the garment. *Be careful* about the iron temperature on the tulle. Make sure the iron is at a low temperature setting, such as silk, wool, or synthetic.

13. Fold and press the lace trim in half. Wrap the trim around the armhole edges, pin in place, and sew with a zigzag stitch from the right side of the vest. (Fig. 12)

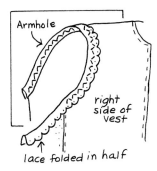

Fig. 12

14. Sew the side seams of the vest. For a split seam, leave a 2" opening at the bottom hem edges. Wrap and sew lace trim around the hem, front openings, and neckline edges of the vest. (Fig. 13) You're done! Now wear and enjoy your vest

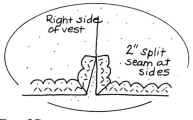

Fig. 13

This project is a great way to recycle a denim shirt and turn it into something very wearable as well as unique. Watch for doilies at yard sales and auctions and let friends and family know you're collecting them for a special project. My neighbor Tona and her sister Mary were very generous with their old doily stashes when they learned what I was doing. I believe that the women who created the doilies years ago would be happy to know their creations are being used and enjoyed, even though not in ways they could have ever predicted.

The next project shows you a way to use the sleeves you cut off the denim shirt.

Teddy Bear Jeans from a Shirt

After I cut apart a denim shirt and made the Doily Vest (page 115), my nephew Matti came to visit with his teddy bears, Simon and Schuster. His mother Becky, one of my nonsewing sisters, had pinned Matti's cut-off blue jeans legs to Simon. Pinned! It looked too cruel to my sister Sarah and me. We were in my sewing parlour and noticed the sleeves I had cut off the denim shirt. We were inspired to turn them into real jeans for poor Simon. The sleeve cuffs became perfect jeans cuffs and, if we do say so ourselves, we thought this idea was quite clever. It turned out to be a great recycling project to share.

Teddy Bear Jeans
This is what happened to the sleeves cut off the denim shirt for the doily vest. The sleeve cuffs are a perfect fit at the bear's ankles and the teddy bear has a classy pair of jeans.

Supplies to Gather:

Teddy bear needing a pair of jeans

2 sleeves with cuffs cut from a denim shirt

Elastic for the waistband, to fit the teddy bear

Steps to Take:

1. Slide the sleeves on the teddy bear legs to determine the inseam length up from the cuffs. Mark the inseam length on each sleeve seam and rip out the stitching to that point of each sleeve. (Fig. 1)

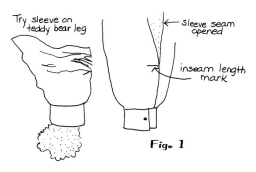

Fig. 1

2. With right sides of the sleeves together, sew the crotch seam by sewing the open sleeve edges together. (Fig. 2)

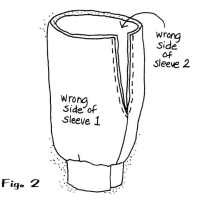

Fig. 2

3. With pants wrong side out, try the pants on the teddy bear. Pin the sides of the pants together to mark a stitching line on the sides of the legs to eliminate extra fabric, unless the teddy bear needs the width. Our medium-size teddy didn't. Sew the side seams and cut away the excess fabric. (Fig. 3)

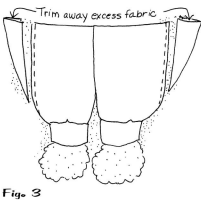

Fig. 3

4. Turn the pants right side out and try them on the teddy bear again, with the cuff openings in the back. Turn under and pin the top edge of the pants for the casing. If the teddy bear has a tail, you'll discover that the back crotch seam needs to be much longer than the seam for the front of the bear. (Fig. 4)

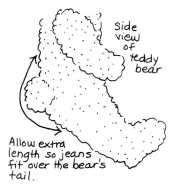

Fig. 4

5. Cut a piece of elastic to fit around the teddy bear's waist. Sew it into a circle. Slide it up inside the fold for the waistline casing and sew the casing closed. (Fig. 5) Your teddy bear now has his/her own new jeans and I hope you have a doily vest made from the rest of the shirt.

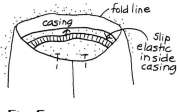

Fig. 5

WORKSHOP

Techniques for Adding Style

In this section, you'll find instruction on techniques that are used several times in this book. It made sense to write them once rather than repeat them for each project.

HOW TO MACHINE APPLIQUE

Button Inspiration Applique
Add an applique to the garment back for an extra-nice touch.

This technique is one of my favorite sewing topics and I've written about it in several other books, including *Mary Mulari Appliques with Style* (see the Resource listing on page 126 for information about all my books). Once you've mastered the basic steps, there's room for your own variations and experimentation. Practice is required; it is the only way I know to perfect satin stitching and other machine applique skills.

Supplies to Gather:

Fabrics for practice - both applique fabric and base fabric

Paper-backed fusible web such as Heat N Bond Lite, Wonder-Under, Aleene's Hot Stitch

Tear-away stabilizer such as Stitch N Tear Pellon, Sulky Tear Easy

Thread to match the applique fabric

Bobbin thread in neutral color or to match the applique

Steps to Take:

1. To practice machine applique, cut the heart shape pattern out of paper and trace the shape on the paper side of paper-backed fusible web. If the design has a definite right and left side, like the letter "B," trace the design backwards. Leaving a narrow margin all around the design, cut it out. Place it, paper side up, on the wrong side of the applique fabric and fuse it in place. (Fig. 1)

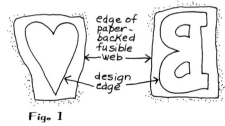

Fig. 1

Pay attention to the instructions for the iron temperature and the length of time to hold the iron on the paper. After the paper has cooled for a few seconds, peel back just one corner of the paper to loosen it from the fabric, then cut the heart shape from the fabric, following the lines drawn on the paper-backed fusible web. Remove the paper backing by pulling away the paper corner you loosened before cutting. (Fig 2)

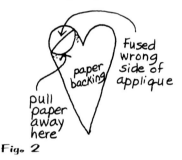

Fig. 2

2. Now the back of your design has a slick surface. Fuse the design in place on the base fabric, positioning the fabric side up and the fused side to the right side of the base fabric.

3. Pin a piece of stabilizer underneath the base fabric. Make sure it is large enough to cover all areas of the design. Now you're ready to sew. (Fig. 3)

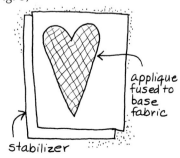

Fig. 3

4. Set the machine for a satin or machine applique stitch. This is a zigzag stitch with a very short stitch length. Try 2.5 width and 0.5 stitch length, and see how well your machine sews this close-together stitch as it covers the raw edge of the applique. Adjust the stitch and width to suit you and your machine. Don't push or pull the fabric, but rest your hands lightly on it to guide it. At the point of the heart, stop with the needle in the fabric and pivot the fabric to continue stitching up the other side. (Fig 4)

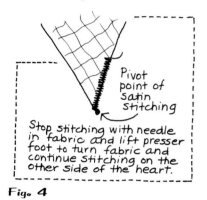

Stop stitching with needle in fabric and lift presser foot to turn fabric and continue stitching on the other side of the heart.

Fig. 4

I suggest overlapping stitches at points to reinforce the stitching. You will also need to stop and pivot the fabric on curved edges. Try to over-lap stitches instead of creating "v" shaped gaps in the stitching line. Remember that the more of these hearts you do, the better you'll get. Practice will make a difference! Try cutting out and stitching more heart appliques and watch your work improve.

5. After completing the stitching and covering the entire edge of the heart, cut the thread ends and pull them to the wrong side of the fabric and knot. Carefully tear away the stabilizer and press your work to flatten it.

6. Many other kinds of applique stitches can be used. A current favorite is the buttonhole or blanket stitch. Notice how many stitches are featured on your machine and take time to try some others too.

HOW TO TRACE PATTERNS FROM GARMENT SECTIONS AND SEW ON NEW FABRIC COVERS

An easy way to add style to many of the garments featured in this book is to cover sections of the garment with other, more interesting fabric. Use this technique to quickly make a pattern piece with seam allowances to cover an area.

Supplies to Gather:

Garment with area to be copied

Tissue or tracing paper large enough for pattern piece

T-pin or pinmarking tool

Steps to Take:

1. Work on a padded surface that will support the portion of the garment to be copied. If working on the ironing board to make a collar tracing, make sure the rest of the garment doesn't drag down the collar.

2. Place a piece of tracing paper on the padded surface. Lay the portion of the garment directly over it. Anchor the garment over the paper by pinning or weighting down the garment with canned goods or sewing weights. It's important that the garment doesn't move once you begin tracing a section.

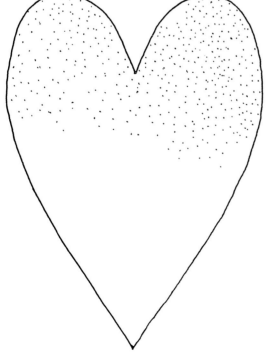

Making a Collar Pattern from a Garment

Pin tracing paper and the garment section to a padded surface. Trace around the collar with a pinmarking tool or T-pin. After removing the garment and tracing paper, add a seam allowance to the traced area on the tissue paper.

3. With a T-pin or pinmarking tool, make pin marks around the edge of the section to be traced. On a collar, the thickest area will be where the collar joins the neckline or the collar-stand. On a heavyweight denim jacket, you may have to press a pin very hard through the jacket fabric to make an impression on the tracing paper. (Fig. 1)

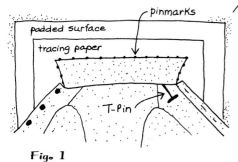

Fig. 1

4. Remove the garment and on the tracing paper, look for the pin holes that mark the actual outline of the section you want to duplicate in other fabric. Draw a line connecting the pin holes. Plan to add seam allowances to the pinmarked lines. (Fig. 2)

Fig. 2

Some projects will suggest a 1/2" seam allowance that may eventually be trimmed if it adds too much bulk. Mark the grainline on the pattern if you want the cover fabric to follow the same grainline direction as the garment.

5. Cut the new pattern, including seam allowances, from fabric. Pin the center of the fabric to the center of the area to be covered. (Fig. 3)

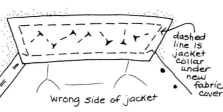

Fig. 3

Use many pins to anchor the fabric and keep it smooth. Turn under and pin the seam allowances to line up with the edges of the section. Sew close to the edges on the right side of the covering fabric to secure the fabric to the garment.

HOW TO REMOVE & REPLACE BUTTONS

Many denim and chambray garments are made with riveted metal buttons and changing them becomes a challenge. I tried many methods of cutting through the button stems only to face frustration and failure. So here's the best way I know to remove riveted buttons and what to do to fix the hole in the garment so you can replace it with a better button.

Supplies to Gather:

Small sharp scissors, such as embroidery scissors

Medium to heavy fabric scraps for covering the hole - Ultra-suede is my favorite

New buttons to replace the old ones

Steps to Take:

1. Insert the point of the scissors into the denim beside the rivet. (Fig. 1) Cut around the rivet, cutting one layer of denim at a time. Eventually you'll have a rivet in your hand and a small hole all the way through the garment.

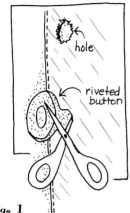

Fig. 1

2. Add fabric pieces to the right and wrong sides of the fabric. (Fig. 2)

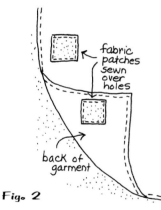

Fig. 2

If the button was removed near a fabric edge, such as on a jacket front, you can wrap one larger piece of fabric around the edge to cover the hole. Use fusible spray or paper-backed fusible web on the wrong side of the fabric to hold it in place, then sew the edges.

3. Now sew a button in place of the old one, making sure the button will fit through the buttonhole. Or change the size of the buttonhole by sewing a patch over the top and cutting the opening through the original buttonhole from the back of the garment. Ultrasuede works very well for buttonhole patches.

4. On many garments featured in this book, I replaced the original buttons that were inexpensive or ordinary. I found that most shirts require nine buttons 1/2" in size, so if you are button shopping and find a good replacement button, remember those numbers. Buttons that are any larger will be difficult to button through shirt buttonholes.

5. Remember that not all buttons have to match. Each one can be different, and that feature alone can add more interest to a garment.

Once you get in the habit of changing buttons, you'll find yourself doing it more often. So many ready-to-wear garments and consignment store treasures look so much better and classier with a change of buttons.

And I can't forget to share my classic button tip about attaching shank buttons with the "golden metallic fasteners" some people call safety pins. (Fig. 3) This removable feature gives you the option of changing your mind about the buttons you want on a garment, or removing them for laundering. If the wrong side of the garment won't be visible, no one will know how you've secured the buttons... it'll be our little secret!

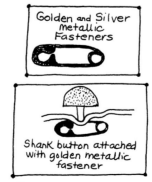

Fig. 3

REMOVING POCKETS – AVOID IT IF YOU CAN!

Many times pockets on shirts and jacket fronts are in the way of a great embellishment technique we have in mind. If removing pockets was a simple matter that took only a few seconds, I'd be the first to recommend it, but there are dangers and difficulties with pocket removal.

Pockets are often heavily stitched with multiple stitching lines and heavy thread tacking on the corners. All of these stitches can be removed, but it is laborious work and a challenge to a seam ripper. Before you begin ripping, find out what the fabric looks like under the pocket. If the garment has been stone-washed or otherwise "distressed" for an aged effect, the fabric inside the pocket could be a very different shade of blue.

Sometimes factories mark pocket stitching places with small holes in the base fabric or permanent dark marks that are impossible to remove. If your garment has been treated to any of these tortures, reconsider removing the pocket. If there are rivets holding the pocket corners, forget about removing the pocket unless you plan to cover the holes that will result from rivet removal.

This book offers lots of options for covering and ignoring pockets. Note the sunflower over the bib pocket on the jumper on page 53, the pockets that became baskets on page 49, and the dressy denim blazer with elegant fabric over its pockets on page 22.

About the Author

Denim and Chambray with Style is the latest in the series of sewing books by author and teacher Mary Mulari. The topic of trimming plain garments is one of Mary's favorites and so far has been featured in ten of her books.

Mary's home with her office and sewing parlour are located in Aurora, Minnesota, in the northeastern Arrowhead region of the state. She develops her ideas and designs by closely observing patterns in nature, artwork, buildings, and fashion. In a previous life, Mary earned a bachelor of science degree from the University

of Minnesota, Duluth, and taught junior high school English and developmental reading. She has also been a retail business owner and an Aurora Library Board member. She is active in her community and serves as co-chair of the annual quilt show for the Pumpkin Fest.

In addition to writing books, Mary travels extensively to present sewing seminars at sewing stores and guild events throughout the U.S. She appears frequently as a guest on PBS television's "Sewing with Nancy" and has taped a three-part series based on the projects in this book.

She has also appeared on "Sew Perfect," "America Sews with Sue Hausmann," and "Handmade by Design" on Lifetime TV. She recently designed automatic applique embroidery cards for Viking Sewing Machine Company and for Cactus Punch.

Readers of this book are welcome to contact Mary by writing to Mary's Productions, Box 87-K2, Aurora, MN 55705, via e-mail: mbmulari@virginia.k12.mn.us, or through her website: www.marymulari.com.

About the Contributors

Dana Bontrager

Dana Bontrager creates the extraordinary in her Pacific Northwest home. Her designs are almost always unusual, often whimsical, and incorporate a variety of material.

In 1984 Dana established a garment design business. She developed several new techniques for garment manufacture and promoted new ideas within the apparel industry. Experimenting and trial and error have led to some of her most unusual designs. Always one to go outside the lines, she takes an unconventional approach to sewing.

She believes in constantly challenging the boundaries of traditional sewing and developing new skills and creativity.

Currently Dana is producing patterns for the Art-to-Wear enthusiast. Unique and eye-catching, the patterns are casual and built on simple lines, allowing the technique and design to become the focus. She recently purchased Pelle's See-Thru Stamp Company and is enjoying creating designs for these unique clear stamps.

Luveta Nickels

Luveta grew up on a ranch near Fort Pierre, South Dakota, and credits her interest in sewing to rural living. At an early age she competed in 4-H and local sewing contests. Soon the appeal of competition was replaced by the lure of creative flair. She spent her entire first paycheck ($18) on fabric and knew then that sewing would be a passion and a career! Her fascination with old blue jeans also developed early. When asked how many jeans she has in her collection, Luveta smiles and says, "Too many to count."

Luveta owns the company, The Junk-Jeans People, and to date has six Junk-Jeans patterns, a book titled *Junk-Jeans Recycled,* and a sewing notion, Space-Tape, which is distributed internationally.

Luveta has made many guest appearances on PBS sewing programs. She is happiest when sharing her recycling ideas with students across the nation. She travels extensively worldwide and demonstrates her techniques to sold-out audiences. Her class attendees have lightheartedly nicknamed her the "Denim Diva."

Luveta and her husband Steve live near Clark, South Dakota, on a working farm/cattle operation.

Resources

The following mail-order sources may help you locate many of the novel sewing supplies and materials featured in this book. If you write to these companies or individuals requesting information, please include a self-addressed stamped envelope and tell them where you learned of their business. I recommend that you first check with your local sewing stores and sources for most supplies. Supporting all of these businesses promotes a thriving sewing community.

Colorful and Distinctive Buttons and Jewelry
JJ Handworks
15429 9th Place West
Lynnwood, WA 98037-2650
425-742-4382
E-Mail: janeschreven@excelonline.com
Internet: www.jjhandworks.com

Creative Sewing Books, Patterns, and Cactus Punch "Automatic Applique" Card with Nature Designs by Mary Mulari
Mary's Productions
Box 87-K2
Aurora, MN 55705
218-229-2804
E-Mail: mbmulari@virginia.k12.mn.us
Internet: www.marymulari.com

Vintage Japanese Kimono Fabrics
Ah! Kimono
16004 N.E. 195th Street
Woodinville, WA 98072-6459
425-482-6485
E-mail: gingko@ahkimono.com
Internet: www.ahkimono.com

Unique Yarns, Ribbons, and Cords for Embellishment
The Yarn Collection
234 Strawberry Village
Mill Valley, CA 94941
1-800-908-9276
E-Mail: mvknit@msn.com

Denim and Chambray Sportswear to Trim
Sunbelt Sportswear
P.O Box 791967
San Antonio, TX 78279-1967
1-800-531-5916

Junk-Jeans Patterns, Supplies, and Books
Luveta Nickels
RR3 Box 105
Clark, SD 57225
605-532-5625
E-Mail: luveta@itctel.com

Purrfection Artistic Wearables by Dana Bontrager
Paw Prints Patterns & Pelle's See Thru Stamps
19618 Canyon Drive
Granite Falls, WA 98252
1-800-691-4293
360-691-4293
E-Mail: dana@purrfection.com
Internet: www.purrfection.com

Shoe and Other Stencils
ReVisions Garment Patterns by Diane Ericson
Box 7404
Carmel, CA 93921
831-659-1989
E-Mail: dericson@redshift.com
Internet: www.revisions-ericson.com

Yarns for Embellishment and Couching
Sally Houk Exclusives
50 Grand Boulevard
Shelby, OH 44875
419-347-7969

Miniature and Regular Doilies, Yo-yos, and More
Wimpole Street Creations
Check on availability at local craft stores or contact
Barrett House
P.O. Box 540585
North Salt Lake, UT 84054-0585
801-299-0700

Denim Bags and Accessories to Trim
Bagworks, Inc.
3301-C South Cravens Rd.
Ft. Worth, TX 76119
817-446-8080
Internet: www.bagworks.com

Catalog of General and Specialty Sewing Supplies
Nancy's Notions
P.O. Box 683
Beaver Dam, WI 53916
1-800-833-0690
Internet: www.nancysnotions.com

Catalog of General and Specialty Sewing Supplies
Clotilde, Inc.
1-800-545-4002
www.clotilde.com

Rubber Stamp and Supply Catalog
ZimPrints, Inc.
340 Rocky Hill Way
Bolivar, TN 38008
Please send $4 for current catalog

Bibliography

Betzina, Sandra. *Fabric Savvy*. Newtown, CT: Taunton Press, Inc., 1999.

Garbers, Debbie and Janet F. O'Brien. *Point Well Taken. The Guide to Success with Needles & Threads*. Marietta, GA: In Cahoots, 1996.

Mulari, Mary. *Mary Mulari Appliques with Style*. Iola, WI: Krause Publications, 1998.

-----. *Mary Mulari's Garments with Style*. Iola, WI: Krause Publications, 1995.

Nickels, Luveta and Cheryl Bittner. *JunkJeans™ Recycled*. Rapid City, SD: CB Nickels Inc., 1997.

Rock, Susan. *Teach Yourself Machine Embroidery*. Iola, WI: Krause Publications, 1996.

Shaeffer, Claire. *Claire Shaeffer's Fabric Sewing Guide*. Iola, WI: Krause Publications, 1989.

Lee National Day Denim

Wear your denim to support a worthy cause. While preparing to tape a "Sewing with Nancy" television series based on this book, I joined the employees of Nancy's Notions on Lee National Denim Day. Wearing denim clothes and donating to the Susan G. Komen Breast Cancer Foundation supports breast cancer research for finding a cure. For more information about Lee National Denim Day, call 1-800-88-8508 or check the website at www.denimday.com.

Index